Yours truly

J. C. Spencer.

THE REVISION

OF THE

STATUTES OF THE STATE OF NEW YORK

AND

THE REVISERS.

AN ADDRESS

DELIVERED BEFORE THE

ASSOCIATION OF THE BAR OF THE CITY OF

NEW YORK,

JANUARY 22, 1889.

—BY—

WILLIAM ALLEN BUTLER.

PUBLISHED FOR THE ASSOCIATION.

NEW YORK AND ALBANY:

BANKS & BROTHERS, LAW PUBLISHERS.

1889.

Lb

INTRODUCTION.

THIS volume, commemorative of the Revisers of the Statutes of the State of New York and their work, owes its origin to the following correspondence and the action of the Association of the Bar of the City of New York subsequently taken in furtherance of the object to which it relates :

NEW YORK, March 1st, 1888.

To the Executive Committee of the Association of the Bar of the City of New York.

GENTLEMEN :—

I have for a long time desired that some suitable and permanent memorial should exist of the Revisers of the Statutes of this State, JOHN DUER, BENJAMIN F. BUTLER and JOHN C. SPENCER. I name them in the order of their appointment.

The signal services they rendered have been illustrated by the course, during more than half a century, of the administration of government and the progress of jurisprudence, not only in this State but also in the other States where the statutory law has been framed on the model of the Revised Statutes, but as time advances and changes in the law are multiplied the distinctive character of this earlier work is in danger of passing out of view.

It has occurred to me that portraits of the Revisers, placed side by side on the walls of the Association would be a fitting commemoration, and that coupled with the presentation of these portraits a succinct account of the work of the Revision, with sketches of the lives and services of the Revisers, might be prepared and published under the supervision and auspices of the Association so as to form an authentic and permanent addition to the literature of the law.

With this in view and with the consent of the representatives of the families of Chief Justice Duer and Mr. Spencer which has been cheerfully accorded, I now propose to present to the Association the portraits of the Revisers as soon as they can be satisfactorily completed and, if approved by the Executive Committee as works of art, the same shall be received by the Association as its property and placed on its walls, and in connection with their acceptance an historical and biographical memorial, as above indicated, and which I will undertake to prepare, shall, subject to like approval, be published in the Association's annual report or otherwise, as may be determined.

Awaiting your action on this proposition, I am

Very truly yours,

WM. ALLEN BUTLER.

ASSOCIATION OF THE BAR,

7 WEST 29TH STREET.

April 2d, 1888.

WILLIAM ALLEN BUTLER, Esq.,

Dear Sir :—

I have the honor to inform you that at the March meeting of the Executive Committee of this Association, your very liberal and acceptable offer to present to the Association portraits of the distinguished Revisers of the N. Y. Statutes together with memorial sketches of their lives and services was received, and that the Committee thereupon on motion of Mr. Olney unanimously

Resolved, That the letter of Mr. Butler be entered on the Minutes, and that the proposition as therein made be accepted with the cordial thanks of the Committee ; that Mr. Butler be requested to prepare the Memorial referred to in his letter, so that it may be read or delivered in the form of an address before the Association at a Special Meeting to be called for that purpose, and that it be referred to a Committee consisting of the President of the Association, the Chairman of this Committee and Mr. Holt, with power to carry this resolution into effect.

Very respectfully yours,

S. SIDNEY SMITH,

Sec'y Ex. Com.

By appointment of the Executive Committee, a Special Meeting of the Association was held on the Evening of January 22, 1889, when the presentation of the portraits of the Revisers to the Association was made in the presence of a number of invited guests. It was accompanied by an address by Mr. Butler embracing a portion of the matter contained in the present volume. The portraits were accepted on behalf of the Association by Mr. Joseph H. Choate its President, and the following minute was adopted :

At a Special Meeting of the Association of the Bar of the City of New York, held at No. 7 West 29th Street, on the 22d day of January, 1889.

Mr. William Allen Butler presented to the Association portraits in oil of John Duer, Benjamin F. Butler and John C. Spencer, the Revisers of the Statutes of the State of New York ; and delivered an address to the Association on the Revisers and their work.

Mr. Francis Lynde Stetson presented the following resolution, which was seconded by Mr. Charles A. Peabody :

Resolved, That the hearty thanks of this Association be tendered to Mr. Butler for the able, instructive and interesting address to which we have just listened, that it be appropriately published under the direction of the Executive Committee, and distributed among the members of the Association, that there be delivered to Mr. Butler, such number of copies as he may desire ; and that Mr. Butler be respectfully invited to give the Association the manuscript of his address for preservation in its Library.

Which was unanimously adopted.

Extract from the Minutes

S. B. BROWNELL,
Recording Secretary.

The Executive Committee having resolved to accompany the work with engravings of the portraits, these have been executed under the supervision of Messrs. Banks & Brothers, whose house has been honorably identified with the Revised Statutes as the publishers of every successive edition, since the first edition, and by whom this volume is published for the Association.

THE REVISION

AND

THE REVISERS.

THE awakened interest of the American people in the men and the events of the time preceding the war for the Union has opened for the historian, the annalist and the biographer, new paths in old fields.

It was natural that with the re-establishment of the National unity, after the stormy period of peril and conflict, there should come, in due season, a great calm, in whose clear atmosphere the whole life of the nation, past and present, would stand out in such sharp outline, and in such varied forms, as to re-invite to its exploration in every part. Especially has the integrity of the Union, as vindicated and made sure by the issue of the great struggle, set in the clearest light the true sovereignty of each State as the organizer and ruler of its own interior social order and development, and made it more than ever the duty of the citizens of each separate commonwealth to make the record of its growth and progress complete and permanent.

This patriotic service is most of all required of the older States, whose earlier annals embody the beginnings of the systems of government which have now overspread the continent.

The Revised Statutes of New York, familiar to us all,

as the body of the written law by which, during the last fifty-eight years, under the various constitutions and as from time to time amended, the government of this State has been administered in all its departments, stand as a landmark of the progress of free government, and the development of the law as a science within the boundaries of our own State.

The lapse of time since the first enactment of the Revised Statutes, the many additions and changes during nearly three score years of rapid growth and new discovery and invention, and the passing away of two generations of men, have tended to obscure the original work, and to lessen the number of the witnesses who can attest its greatness.

This Association has deemed it fitting that some commemoration of both the work of the Revision and its authors should find a place on these walls and in our records, and it has been for me altogether a privilege, and in part, a filial duty, too long delayed, to provide the portraits of JOHN DUER, BENJAMIN FRANKLIN BUTLER and JOHN CLINTON SPENCER, the three Revisers, for preservation here as a memento of their joint labors in the work which unites their names and memories.

These portraits speak for themselves. Necessarily, no one of them is from life. They are, however, from the best sources available to me with the aid of the relatives of Chief Justice Duer and of Mr. Spencer.

The portrait of Chief Justice Duer is an original by Mr. J. Carroll Beckwith, that of Mr. Spencer is also an original by Mr. William M. J. Rice, while the third portrait is a copy by Howard Russell Butler, faithfully reproduced from an original in my possession, by Thomas Hicks.

They have been approved by the Executive Committee as works of art, worthy of acceptance as the property of the Association.

The Executive Committee have also intrusted me with the task of preparing a sketch, historical as to the revision, and biographical as to the Revisers, to be published under the auspices of the Association as a further permanent memorial of both.

In performing this duty I am reminded that it was accepted more than thirty years ago by the sole surviving Reviser, and its accomplishment prevented by his death shortly afterwards. Mr. Marshall S. Bidwell in his address at the meeting of the Bar held in reference to that event, December 1, 1858, said :

" Upon the occasion which last convened the members of the Bar—the death of Judge Duer—Mr. Butler made an address which will be remembered by all those present ; at the conclusion of that meeting, I expressed a wish to him that, as he was the sole survivor of the gentlemen concerned in that labor, he would reduce to writing a statement of the manner in which it was accomplished, and the different parts the Revisers took in it. He expressed his willingness, if it was the desire of the members of the Bar, to do so. On enquiry I found it was, as I anticipated, the general desire of the Bar, and I had taken measures to have it accomplished when he was obliged to depart for Europe."

As the circumstances seem thus to have devolved this duty upon me as a special obligation, its discharge, however inadequate, will, I trust, be accepted as an effort to furnish a record not unworthy of a place in the history and literature of the law.

The place of New York in the Union of the States was originally determined and has been maintained by lawyers. Within her boundaries, on her Bench and at her Bar, there have always been jurists of integrity, ability and patriotism, devoted to the task of creating and administering her free government.

The Dutch colony of New Netherland, dating from 1614, and continuing for half a century, adopted the system of townships and magistracies derived from the institutions of Holland, whose local municipal system, under the government of the States General, embodied the theory of Republican Government. Under this system the people were trained in the rudimental ideas of representative government and on the establishment of the English rule in March, 1664, the population, although not then exceeding ten thousand souls, were impatient of external control, and ready to assert and maintain popular rights.

The English Colonial rule proceeded on the assumption of absolute control in the Crown. No charter was ever granted to the colonists; the Governor and Colonial Council of seven members, afterwards increased to twelve, were commissioned by the King, and the General Assembly was chosen by the freeholders of the several counties, but the Governor had an absolute veto on all bills passed by the Assembly and Council, and also the power of proroguing and dissolving the Assembly. All laws passed by the Colonial Legislature were subject to approval or rejection by the King, and if disapproved were void.

This semblance of a representative government, made more intolerable by the oppression of Parliament, culminating in the Stamp Act, was thrown off by the Revolution, and the State of New York came into existence under the Constitution of April 20, 1777.

This Constitution, the fifth of the series of Constitutions adopted by the States, was drawn by John Jay, afterwards the first Chief Justice of the Supreme Court of the United States, as chairman of the committee to whom its preparation was intrusted.

Robert R. Livingston, the first Chancellor, William Smith, one of the ablest jurists of his time, John Sloss Hobart and Robert Yates, the first *puisné* Judges of the Supreme Court, Gouverneur Morris and William Duer, father of the Reviser, were conspicuous members of this committee.

The Constitution declared that "such parts of the common law of England and of Great Britain and of the acts of the Colonial Legislature as together formed the law of the colony at the breaking out of the Revolution in 1775, constituted the law of the State, subject to alteration by the Legislature."

The Colonial Laws from 1691 to 1777, inclusive, had been the subject of several revisions and additions. The Laws of the State were edited and revised in 1789, under the direction of the Legislature, by Samuel Jones and Richard Varick, and later, in 1801, by Chief Justice Kent and Justice Radcliff of the Supreme Court. In 1813, another revision was made by William P. Van Ness and John Woodworth, known as the Revision of 1813.

None of these so-called revisions was anything more than a mere re-enactment in a consolidated form of the existing statutes as they had been passed from time to time, with some amendments suggested by the Revisers or inserted by the Legislature. They were drawn in separate acts with no attempt at systematic arrangement.

They were all similar to the earlier revisions made during the Colonial period, first by William Smith and William Livingston in 1762, and afterwards by Peter Van Schaick in 1774.

Thus the first general statute in the two volumes of the Revised Laws of 1813 is one passed in 1784 in relation to magistrates who may take affidavits, and the last is one passed in 1813 to prevent trespasses on Indian Lands. Between these are inserted, in chronological order, but otherwise without any attempt at classification, the many hundred statutes of the intermediate years as modified by amendments or other changes in the law.

In 1821 the Constitution was amended and again the leading lawyers of the State controlled the convention. Chancellor Kent, Martin Van Buren, Ambrose Spencer, Peter A. Jay, John Duer, Erastus Root and Henry Wheaton were among the members of the body. Radical changes were made in the organic law and in the mode of administering the government, and soon after the new Constitution went into effect, January 1, 1823, it became evident that these changes as well as those made by the successive Legislatures since 1813, necessitated a new revision of the statutes.

Governor Yates had been a Judge of the Supreme Court from 1808 to 1822 and by his judicial experience had become familiar with the defects of the existing statutes. He urged the subject upon the Legislature and an act was passed, November 27, 1824, appointing James Kent, Erastus Root, then Lieutenant-Governor, and Benjamin F. Butler, to revise the statutes of the State. The act required the work to be completed in two years and provided for a compensation of one thousand dollars each for the services to be performed by the Revisers.

This act contemplated a revision similar to those of 1813 and former years. It did not authorize anything beyond the compilation of the existing statutes in the manner pursued in the earlier revisions, much less a remodelling of the statutory law or the reduction to statutory form of the Common Law.

JAMES KENT, whose name stood at the head of the commission thus constituted, had retired, July 31, 1823, from the office of Chancellor. He had served the State as one of the *puisné* Judges of the Supreme Court, from his first appointment February 6, 1798, to July 2, 1804, when he became Chief Justice and so remained until February 25, 1814, the date of his appointment as Chancellor. His judicial career had placed him on the roll of great Judges, and the wonderful revolution in the practice and administration of equity accomplished during the nine years of his service as Chancellor is attested by the tributes paid him by the Bar on his retirement and which occupy the concluding pages of the final volume of Johnson's Chancery Reports.

This brilliant career on the Bench was cut short at the age of sixty years, by the operation of the provision in the Constitution of 1821, which perpetuated a similar provision in the Constitution of 1777, disqualifying the higher judicial officers from the exercise of their duties after attaining sixty years of age.

The first draft of the judiciary article of the Constitu
tion of 1821 extended the tenure of the judicial officers to
seventy years of age, but by some sinister influence the un-
reasonable limitation of sixty years was substituted by
the convention. Denounced in strong terms by Hamilton,
in the Federalist, as early as 1778,* its reappearance
in the new Constitution was justly declared to be
" a satire on the intellect of the Bar and a standing re-
proach to the discernment and integrity of the appointing
power.† "

Driven from the Bench at the height of his judicial fame
and in the fullness of his judicial capacity, it was incom-
patible with the views of the ex-Chancellor, governed as
they probably were, by the prevailing ideas of the period,
that he should resume practice at the Bar. He said to
James I. Roosevelt, then a young man, long afterwards a
Judge of the Supreme Court, in our city, " I would rather
saw wood." Judge Roosevelt, in relating to me this incident, added that he himself suggested to Chancellor Kent
the preparation of a work on Equity jurisprudence, an
idea amplified and improved upon in the noble task to
which he addressed himself, whose splendid issue in the
Commentaries on American Law have more than healed the
wound inflicted by the blunder or the crime of the Constitution makers of 1821.

Chancellor Kent, in a manner entirely characteristic,
declined to act as one of the Revisers. While the question
of his acceptance was pending, a rumor was started by the
gossip mongers, of whom the political circles were
as full then as they are now, that he was unwilling to
be associated with the Commissioner whose name was last
on the list, because of some strictures he had made in the
Court of Errors on one of the Chancellor's decrees, and it
was doubtless thought a very probable circumstance,
at a time when judges and lawyers were alike partisan and

---

* Federalist, No. 79.
† 7 John's Chy. R., p. 347, note.

prejudiced to an extent we can hardly understand and happily do not emulate, that the antagonism in the political views of the veteran Federalist Chancellor and a young and ardent Republican lawyer, the political associate of Tompkins and Van Buren, might well be an additional obstacle to their serving together on the commission.

It turned out that the Chancellor had been wholly misrepresented as to this supposed ground of reluctance to accept the appointment. He was willing to serve, but he did not want any associate. He wrote under date of November 29, 1824, as follows :

" BENJAMIN F. BUTLER, Esq.,

Dear Sir.—I beg leave to assure you that Mr. C. is wholly mistaken in supposing there is any personal difference between you and me, or that I should for that cause be unwilling to be associated with you. I have the highest confidence in the purity and honor that govern you, and I can scarcely recollect anything of the occurrence which was the foundation of the supposed misunderstanding. I have only a faint recollection of something having been said by you in the Court of Errors, relative to the errors of one of my Chancery decrees, which as reported to me in the first instance, gave me some pain. But the explanation followed immediately afterwards and was entirely satisfactory, and I have not thought of the matter since. I have no other feeling towards you than those of strong respect and esteem.   *   *

I am your Friend & ob't Ser't
JAMES KENT."

A few days later, December 8th, 1824, after having formally declined the appointment, he again wrote as follows : " It would have been most convenient to me to have had the duty of revising the laws assigned to me alone, giving me a reasonable time and allowing me a reasonable compensation, but if it was thought best to have an associate that was agreeable to me I should have had no objection and you would have been entirely and perfectly agreeable to me as an associate."

It was fortunate for the work of the Revision, as finally developed, that Chancellor Kent declined to take part in it. As the sole Reviser, he would have been more than competent for the task, which would have been mainly a repetition of his earlier work in conjunction with Judge Radcliff, in 1801, but while his long exercise of undivided authority as Chancellor made him averse to working with associates, his still longer exercise of the judicial function had unfitted him for sympathy and co-operation in the bold and novel methods for which the Revision gave the opportunity and which demanded the enthusiasm and courage of men of a new generation.

A quarter of a century passed on the Bench, in the application of the rules of the English Common Law and the English Court of Chancery to the affairs of a new commonwealth which, while it gloried in its independence as a State, held fast to the systems of law and equity of the mother country, with a tenacity which independence seemed only to strengthen, was an admirable preparation for the task of a commentator whose work is mainly retrospective, but not for the architect of an improved system of jurisprudence.

John Duer was appointed by Governor Yates to fill the place vacated by Chancellor Kent. He accepted with alacrity and, as the speedy result of the concurring views of himself and his junior colleague, a bold and radical change was made by them in the whole scheme of the Revision and the methods of its execution.

By that kind of inspiration which so often waits on true devotion to a high calling, the idea came to them of replacing the mass of disconnected statutes they were called upon to collate by a new and complete system of original laws, regulating every department of government, based upon the old foundations of the common law and the existing statutes, and made serviceable by fundamental and far reaching changes and by a symmetrical and scientific arrangement.

This rare opportunity they seized with that unquestioning enthusiasm which, when rightly directed and controlled, is the surest presage of success.

To set this new movement in operation far greater powers were needed by the Revisers than those conferred by the appointing Act of 1824, and, immediately upon the assembling of the Legislature of 1825, which convened on the fourth day of January, we find the two junior Revisers in communication with the Assembly, stating, very modestly but with absolute clearness, the plan they proposed and asking for the needed grant of power for its execution.

They advanced the proposition that the time had come when the whole written law might be comprised under appropriate titles, classified in natural order and arranged, as to each of its branches, in a clear and scientific method and, while conceding the novelty and difficulty of the project, declared their readiness to undertake it.

Their statement was accompanied by a specimen of the new style of statute by which they sought to replace the old and cumbrous system of Revision. This specimen embodied the statutory regulation of the Court of Errors and the Court of Chancery.

Placed side by side with the existing statutes on the same subject the comparison showed at a glance the vast advantage to be gained by reduction in length, in simplification of expression and in the scientific co-relation of all the parts to the whole which was the key to the entire system as proposed. In connection with this profert by way of sample, they urged the importance of redeeming the laws from the uncertainties and obscurities arising from the intricate and obsolete diction in which so many of them, especially those copied from the English acts, had been written and the advantage of establishing the whole body of the statute law in such permanent form that instead of constantly recurring Revisions, particular amendments and additions could be made as occasion might require, without disturbing the other parts of the system.

They add :

" We are fully aware of the responsibility that we incur by proposing to the legislature a new mode of conducting a Revision of the laws, and are prepared to encounter the charge, so easily preferred, of rash and unnecessary innovation. In reply to such a charge, we shall only observe, that the conviction of the practicability and great importance of the change which we recommend, has been produced in our own minds by slow and careful deliberation, overcoming the prepossessions common to the profession to which we belong.

That much care, diligence and research will be requisite to the successful execution of this plan, we freely admit, and it is with a full sense of the difficulties it may impose upon ourselves, that we urge its adoption ; yet we trust we may without presumption express our belief that these difficulties may be overcome, the evils which may be apprehended effectually obviated, and the advantages which we have endeavored to indicate, to a considerable extent be secured and realized.

We solicit a comparison of the acts drawn up by us, with those now in force, of which they are Revisions. After such a comparison   *   *   *   it will be found that we propose to do nothing more than to free our written code from the prolixities, uncertainties and confusion, incident to the style and manner in which it has hitherto been framed, and to apply to the elucidation of this branch of the noblest of all sciences, those principles of an enlarged philosophy, which now obtain in every other department of knowledge."

It will be noticed that General Root did not unite in this communication, nor did he ally himself to the advanced methods of his colleagues. An active and veteran party leader and an able advocate of the older type, he was neither adapted nor inclined to the work of a pioneer in legal reform. He had already since his appointment done something at his home in Delaware County towards Revising, in the old fashioned way, the laws relating to taxes and to highways, subjects always interesting to the rural legislator, but the change of plan on which his associates had resolved led to his retirement, and the new bill giving the Revisers ampler powers, substituted Henry Wheaton in his place and provided for a compensation of $500 to Gen. Root for the services he had rendered.

This new bill was not passed without a struggle. It was at first laid on the table by the Assembly by a vote of 54 to 51, and finally passed by a vote of 56 to 38. Nothing which involved a delegation or an exercise of public powers could be accomplished in those days of bitter political conflict without a struggle between the Clintonians, whose great leader had just been elected Governor, and the Bucktails, as the Democrats of the day were dubbed.

In the Senate, John C. Spencer, then a member of that body, afterwards one of the Revisers, moved to amend by striking out Mr. Wheaton's name and committing the whole work to the two acting Revisers, Messrs. Duer and Butler. This was voted down. It was then moved to increase the compensation of General Root, who had been the presiding officer of the preceding Senate, from $500 to $1,000. This was carried and for a time imperiled the whole measure. The Assembly thought $500 ample compensation for a few months work, for which a thousand dollars for two years service was the stipulated price. It refused to concur in the Senate's amendment; the Senate refused to recede; finally a conference committee adjusted the difference, the higher measure of compensation was conceded and the bill as finally passed, April 2, 1825, gave the retiring Reviser a thousand dollars which must be placed to the debit of the general tax system and the turnpikes and other highways of the State.

The new Act allowed two years for the completion of the work, and while fixing the same compensation as the former Act, provided that it might be increased by the Legislature.

Whatever questions had arisen as to the wisdom of

entering on the unexampled movement of reform authorized by the Act of 1825, none had been raised as to the competency of the two men who had initiated it and who volunteered to carry it to completion.

JOHN DUER, born at Albany, October 7, 1782, a son of Colonel William Duer, of Revolutionary memory, had, after two years' service in the United States Army, which he joined at the age of sixteen years, entered the office of General Hamilton. The deficiency of his early education he made good by a thorough course of study, particularly in the classics and the modern languages, preparatory to entering on the special study of the law. As early as 1816 we find him acting as counsel in the Court of Errors, associated with John V. Henry and opposed by Thomas J. Oakley and Martin Van Buren, in the important case of Jackson *vs*. DeLancey, reported in 13 Johnson, which involved the title to lands in the city of New York, once the property of his maternal grandfather, William Alexander, the Lord Stirling of the revolutionary army. He was at that time practising law in Orange County, and was firmly established in a leading position at the Bar. He came into prominent public life as a delegate from Orange County to the Convention of 1821, in which he distinguished himself by his ability and eloquence. He had acquired a reputation, justly accorded and never impaired during his long and active life, for "great quickness and fertility of intellect, and for a vast amount of acquired knowledge not merely in the learning of his profession, but in kindred sciences and general literature." His mind had a wide range without being weakened by its discursive habit. The more recondite the subjects of legal investigation the more they attracted him, and the remodelling of the law was a task kindred and congenial to his intellect.

BENJAMIN F. BUTLER, a native of Columbia County, N. Y., was born December 14, 1795, at Kinderhook Landing, on the Hudson, afterwards set off as a separate town

by the name of Stuyvesant. He came of an original Irish
stock, combined with that of the early Puritans by the
marriage of his ancestor, Jonathan Butler, with Temperance Buckingham, a daughter of one of the first settlers of
Connecticut.

His father, Medad Butler, emigrated from Branford,
Connecticut, in 1787, at the age of twenty-two, to the
banks of the Hudson, where he established himself in
business, and where he lived during the rest of his life of
eighty-four years, serving the State during a part of it in
the Legislature, and for many years as a county judge of
Columbia County. Of a family of twelve children, six of
whom died in infancy, the Reviser was the eldest.

Educational advantages were almost unknown in this
State in the earlier part of this century, outside of its more
thickly settled portions, and the Dutch settlers of Kinderhook did not include the schoolmaster in their municipal
arrangements. To a native of New England who had
enjoyed the benefit of the schools already planted there,
the want of like facilities for his children was a sore trial.
By a happy accident the need was amply supplied. Two
young men, John Freese and Elijah Garfield by name, came
from Stockbridge, Mass., to Kinderhook Landing, bound
for New York, and asked for passage on one of Medad
Butler's sloops. He found that their voyage was with the
intent of establishing themselves as schoolmasters on Long
Island, where they hoped to find employment in some of
the older settlements. He at once tried to persuade them
to tarry at the "Landing" and set up a school there,
specially for the benefit of the bright pupil he could
furnish in his eldest boy, who had shown a wonderful love
of reading and study. The young men were, however,
bent on pushing their way southward, but agreed that, in
case of the failure of their plan, they would return and
accept the offer. Long Island did not prove the land of
promise they had looked for, and before many days they
re-appeared, and, true to their word, started the school at
the "Landing."

Both these men were good teachers, and inspired their young pupil with a love of the classics he never lost. He read Latin as a habit almost daily during his life, carrying in his vest pocket a leaf torn from an old edition of his favorite Horace, employing his spare moments while waiting in Court, or at other chance periods of leisure, in reading and re-reading, and sometimes turning into English verse, the numbers of the Roman poet.

Garfield, a type of the old style pedagogue, taught school all his life, and for many years at Middletown, Connecticut, where he prepared boys for college. After his favorite pupil had fulfilled all his early promise, and risen to the highest rank in his profession and to prominence in public service, he made a visit to the school of his old preceptor, whom he found engaged as of yore in the drudgery of the recitation room. Overjoyed at the appearance of his old-time pupil, he threw aside his text book and ferule, dismissed the school, and sent the boys off happy in an unexpected half-holiday.

On leaving school in 1811, the young student went into the office, at Hudson, of Martin Van Buren, a warm personal friend of his father, who saw such signs of promise in the son that he pressed him into his closest service. Until his marriage in 1818, he was an inmate of Mr. Van Buren's family, his law partner in Albany from the time of his admission to the Bar in 1817, and the successor, in large measure, of the legal business from which Mr. Van Buren withdrew on his election to the United States Senate in 1821.

Mr. Van Buren's standing and repute as a lawyer were greater than is generally supposed. His later conspicuous public career, culminating in the Presidency, has obscured his earlier brilliant record as a lawyer. In fact, he was, during his active practice and until his exclusive devotion to public affairs, at the very front of the Bar, succeeding Abraham Van Vechten and preceding Thomas J. Oakley as Attorney-General of the State at a time when leadership in the profession was an essential qualification for the place, and competing in forensic struggles with the ablest advocates. The terse and frank admission of his great rival, Elisha Williams, the incomparable jury lawyer of his time, that, while he got all the verdicts, Van Buren got all the judgments, was only a fair tribute to his ascendency. Tardy justice is being done to Mr. Van Buren as jurist, statesman and patriot, and it is to the honor of our Association that one of its members, in a recent biography marked by absolute candor, thorough research, and a rare literary skill, has rescued his memory from the disparagement and detraction of prejudiced and superficial writers of opposing political views, and set it in a true historic light.

Mr. Van Buren had no misgiving in committing to his young partner in the law the care of his clients and their causes. In fact, the junior was already established on his own merits. In illustration of this, I may be permitted to quote from a biographical sketch published in January, 1839, fifty years ago, a passage which describes his first appearance in the Court of Errors, which runs as follows :

" He was the attorney in a cause, with Colonel Burr and Mr. Van Buren, against the celebrated Mr. Henry, then at the head of the Albany Bar, and one of the most eminent lawyers in the State. The case turned on recondite questions of black-letter learning, and such was the impression made by Mr. Butler's argument, that neither of his distinguished senior counsel thought it worth while to speak in the cause, which was gained single-handed by the young advocate whose first effort was thus so arduous and so honorable. His first cause in the Court of Errors was also won, in the next year, in a similar single combat with the same powerful antagonist. Mr. Van Buren who had argued it in the Supreme Court below, having, on his withdrawal from practice, advised his client to entrust it to Mr. Butler's hands. This success placed him at once in the front rank of his profession."

In 1821 he was appointed District Attorney of Albany

County, and was the incumbent of that office when, most unexpectedly to himself and also to Mr. Duer, as he declared in his eulogy on the Chief Justice at the meeting of the Bar of this city, held August 6, 1858, they were appointed Revisers. The casual intimacy they had formed as associates in a cause at the Columbia Circuit, was thus suddenly cemented into a close alliance.

On his resignation from the office of District Attorney in March, 1825, the Court of Common Pleas, by an entry in its minutes, paid an unusually warm tribute to the fairness as well as the fidelity with which he had discharged his duties as a public prosecutor.

When appointed Reviser, he lacked seventeen days of being twenty-nine years of age.

We thus find the task of re-framing the whole statute law of the State upon a new and untried basis, committed mainly, and on their own motion, to two young men who had sprung from the ranks of the people, neither of whom held a college diploma, both of whom had carved their own way to leadership, and who, while their elders shrank from this task, had courted it themselves with that consciousness of strength and mastery which the world of smaller men sometimes calls self-conceit, but which is so often, in the individual aspirant, only the healthy beating of the pulse of genius.

The Legislature, by the Act of 1825, as we have seen, probably at the suggestion of the two other Revisers, had named Henry Wheaton as their associate. He had been a member, with John Duer, of the Constitutional Convention of 1821, and at the time of his appointment as Reviser was the reporter of the Supreme Court of the United States, an office he held until January, 1827. In April of that year, he was sent as Chargé d'Affaires of the United States to Denmark, and ceased to act in the Revision.

In the correspondence of the Revisers in my possession there is no trace of any considerable work done by Mr.

Wheaton in conjunction with his colleagues, although his name appears with theirs, appended to the Revisers' reports to the Legislatures of 1826 and 1827. He prepared one or two of the earlier chapters, but, probably, besides this did little more than to concur in the action of his associates. But, at the outset, he gave to their plan his hearty assent, and while no letters or memoranda by him are included in the papers of the revision, one important document exists which, by a few words of endorsement in his unmistakable handwriting and phraseology, establishes the authorship and the date of the first written plan of the entire work. This paper of eleven pages of the coarse unruled foolscap of the time, is entitled "General Arrangement," and contains a sketch and outline of all that was afterwards embodied in the Revised Statutes, classifying the entire body of laws for the government of the State, under five leading heads. Prepared immediately after the passage of the Act of April 21, 1825, it brings into outline the work as it lay in the minds of the promoters of that act, and is a summary of the system they sought to establish.

It starts by dividing under five leading heads, the whole body of the law.

1. The laws which relate to the government, to the general policy, and to the internal police of the State.

2. The laws which relate to the domestic relations, to property, to contracts, and to other matters connected therewith.

3. The laws which relate to the judiciary establishments, and to the mode of procedure in civil cases.

4. The laws relating to crimes and punishments, and to the mode of prosecution and punishment.

5. Local Laws.

Then follows a subdivision of Chapters, Titles and Articles, giving the particulars of the laws to be classified under each of the five general divisions as proposed, beginning with the boundaries of the State and its territorial divisions, and the regulation of government of counties and towns, and proceeding to cover the whole subject of governmental control in all its departments, upon the system which, as perfected, was embodied in the Revised Statutes. This paper is endorsed, "Projet of General Plan of Revision handed in by Mr. Butler, May 11, 1825."

The entire paper is in the handwriting of the Reviser who thus "handed in" and submitted to the judgment of his colleagues what, probably, Mr. Wheaton alone of the New York lawyers of his day would have thought of designating a *projet*, a word which his habits of study as a civilian and a publicist suggested to him as best descriptive of such novel and far reaching propositions. In this term, and in the marginal suggestions which he made, we find one of those incidental traits which reveal, by a casual touch, the individual character and distinct personality of the writer. Mr. Wheaton's reputation stands on his earlier work as a reporter of the Supreme Court during the period to which belong the great constitutional arguments and decisions, in the time of Chief Justice Marshall, so fully exhibited in the twelve volumes of his reports, and on his later work as a commentator on International Law. His almost life-long voluntary exile, in a diplomatic service, first at Copenhagen, and then at Berlin, withdrew him from his profession and from the society of his countrymen, to whom he is known only as an author. It would doubtless have been a pleasing anticipation, could he have foreseen that the few words of endorsement traced by his hand on the discolored manuscript now first produced, after the lapse of more than three score years, before a body of lawyers in the chief city of the nation, would identify the earliest recorded effort at a written system of governmental statute law for an English-speaking people.

While the manuscript, both by the handwriting of the body of the plan and by Mr. Wheaton's endorsement, shows by whom it was prepared, it must be understood that no claim is made to exclusive originality in the ideas it embodies. On the contrary, the author of the plan himself in the address already referred to, in commemoration of Chief Justice Duer, whose death was within a few months to be followed by his own, generously accorded the merit of the first suggestion of the plan to the friend whom he eulogized.

Without detracting from the force of this concession, the fact remains that the initial step in the revision, by which form was first given to the idea of a work so unprecedented, so delicate and so difficult, is found in this draft, and it is not unworthy of notice that the original conception of his associates, and his own matured views were thus traced by a young lawyer, not then thirty years old, in the first decade of his practice at the Bar, with no other experience than that gained in his native State, and in the face of the adverse sentiment of the profession.

It is almost impossible for the men of this generation, who have been trained in the system which the Revised Statutes established, and accustomed to the organic law as established by the Constitution of 1846 and subsequent amendments, and the various codes which have been adopted and projected, and who are also accustomed to innovations, experiments and schemes in every department of our many-sided social system, to comprehend the state of things existing on May 11, 1825, the date of the first draft of the plan of the Revised Statutes.

Not only the so-called "black-letter" lawyers whose professional horizon was limited by the metes and bounds of the Common Law, but the great body of jurists on the Bench and at the Bar were firm in their adhesion to the legal methods of the mother country. They were more than satisfied with the common law as it had been moulded to meet the expanding needs of civilization and commerce by Lord Mansfield and with the system of equity jurisprudence which had been worked out through the long line of eminent Chancellors, of whom Lord Eldon, then on the wool-sack was the last, and in whom the genius of reform never found a more consistent opponent. Many of the leading lawyers of New York were by training and family and political association tenacious of established customs and violently opposed to change and to men given to change. The idea of codification, although in comparison with the cyclonic proportions it has since assumed, a cloud no bigger than a man's hand, was in the air, a baleful portent. Civilians were multiplying in the ranks of jurists in England and in the United States. De Witt Clinton, whose genius was allied to commercial enterprise, favored a code in his message at the opening of the year 1825. He declared that "the whole system of our jurisprudence requires revised arrangement and correction. A complete code founded on the salutary principles of society, adapted to the interests of commerce and the useful arts, the state of society and the nature of our government, and embracing those improvements which are enjoyed by enlightened experience, would be a public blessing. It would free our laws from uncertainty, elevate a liberal and honorable profession and utterly destroy judicial legislation, which is fundamentally at war with the principles of representative government."

While the Tory journals were inveighing against the innovators who would sacrifice everything that was ancient and venerable on their "shrine of simplicity" and declaring that the word "code" had something imperial and arbitrary in its sound which grated on the ears of a disciple of Bracton or Littleton, the Edinburgh *Review* called attention to the fact that New York had "resumed with increasing patience its habitual work of reform;"* and while the commission appointed by Parliament in 1824 had only recommended some measures of reform for consideration, the Revisers were accomplishing in fact what in England was merely discussed as theory.

Against these innovating tendencies the whole body of the profession was arrayed. The plan of the Revised Statutes was devised in the presence of a sentiment which

---

*Edinburgh *Review*, March, 1827, p 481.

warned the Revisers that any attempt to import Continental or civil law methods into the jurisprudence of the State, would be an act of treason to the Bench and the Bar. They could hardly escape the suspicion of being at least infected with these treasonable projects and with a disposition to give aid and comfort to their abettors. Fortunately they had the spirit of reformers without the rage of iconoclasts. They publicly declared that their work was not intended to be codification. Their earliest report to the Legislature says that "the practicability and advantages of reducing the Common Law of England to a written code has recently been maintained in that country by several writers. In this country, also, similar opinions have been advanced by some of our ablest jurists, and we think those opinions are gradually gaining ground in both countries. On the other hand, a majority of the legal profession in each is averse to the scheme." To codify the whole law or any branch of it in the sense of substituting positive written definitions and enactments for the law as existing in the common law and equity systems and as interpreted and applied by the Courts, was never the intention or aim of the Revisers, or any one of them. They publicly declared that the work they had in charge "must be carefully distinguished from codification. * * We have found it necessary in our report to exclude this idea which has got abroad and exposed us to much prejudice with those who believe every project of that sort visionary and dangerous."

To use the formula employed by an inventor in asserting and describing, for the purpose of securing a patent, the substance of what he supposes to be new and useful in his invention, what I claim on behalf of the authors of the project of the Revision, as exhibited in the original paper of May 11, 1825, is, that it was the first attempt to create and establish for any commonwealth governed by the English Common Law, and by legislative statutes, after the manner of the English Parliament, of a body of written law, systematically arranged, based on the principles of the law as a science, regulating the exercise of public and private rights, establishing domestic, property and contract relations, and covering the administration of every department of the Government, without touching the integrity of the unwritten law, or transcending the proper bounds of legislative control. More than this, it was the first attempt to so organize the statute law of an English-speaking race, as to retain and apply all the great and beneficial principles of the Common Law, while rejecting and casting off those parts of it which were alien to the genius of a State in which the feudal system of England had never taken root, or been transplanted and where free institutions were in revolt against its old abuses.

The general plan having been settled upon, the Revisers immediately entered on the work of preparing for the coming session of the Legislature. The first installment of their work was intended to present an outline of the entire plan, and to embrace the initial chapters of the Revision.

During the summer of 1825, Mr. Duer, who was engaged in New York on Chapter V, relating to Elections, wrote on August 23, to his colleague at Albany, enclosing the chapter, and saying: "In compiling it, I am sensible I have carried, to their full extent, the powers that the Legislature have given us. I have, however, made no changes or additions for which there did not appear a sufficient reason to my own mind, but to explain the reasons would require a dissertation, and I prefer leaving the subject without any remarks of my own, to your unprejudiced judgment, and I beg you to examine the whole with care and criticise with freedom. If you are satisfied with the plan and arrangement, then direct your minute attention to the style and diction, and mark every ambiguous, obscure, improper and superfluous sentence, phrase, or word. Let us act and labor under the belief that we are working for posterity, and that great results are dependent (as I am convinced they are) upon our success." He adds that he is going on with Chapter II, which he says "will give me more occupation than I expected."

His Albany colleague was meanwhile employed on

Chapter I, which according to the orderly plan of arrangement was to treat of the boundaries of the State and its territorial jurisdiction.

"It is a singular fact," noted by the Revisers, in reporting this chapter that "no complete account of the bounds of the State, as now established and claimed, is to be found in any printed work or public record." The sources of a correct description of the territory of the State included royal patents and charters, and conventions with neighboring States, and other public documents. With the assistance of the Surveyor General, the metes and bounds of the Empire State, as actually in possession of its sovereign people, were for the first time ascertained and defined.

This formed the initial chapter of the Revised Statutes, an adaptation, to some extent, of the Domesday Acts, and of the descriptions of the possessions of the twelve tribes of Israel given in the Book of Joshua.

Then followed, by way of exception, a title describing the places ceded by the State of New York to the United States. The second chapter embraced similarly minute descriptions of the civil divisions of the State, the Counties, Senatorial and Congressional districts, towns and cities. Most of these were, however, published as local acts, by way of addition to the third volume of the Statutes, so as not to encumber the main work with formal matters.

The Legislature of 1826 met on the 3d day of January. The Revisers were alive to the importance of making their first report in such form as to create a favorable impression on the members of both Houses. A letter to Messrs. Duer and Wheaton, from their associate, dated January 18, 1826, says: "As the report would be, to us at least, an important document, great pains should be taken in drawing it up. Our best faculties must be put in requisition and I have sketched, and now enclose to you, an outline of the topics to be discussed in it."

Mr. Duer wrote in reply: "the task of preparing our report seems to devolve *ex-necessitate* on yourself." The report was accordingly prepared and submitted March 14, 1826. It contains the first public announcement of the plan of the Revision, and gives a clear analysis of the various subjects to be embraced in the scope of a complete system of public Statutory Law, marking out the general division into Parts, and the subdivision into Chapters, and Titles as indicated in outline in the original plan of May 11, 1825, thus placing clearly before the Legislature and the public the idea of a systematic body of Statutory Law, to be permanent in its form, and all-embracing in respect to the administration of the Government in its various departments. The report presented only Chapter V "Of Elections, other than for Town Officers" but with full details of the intended character of the work of which that chapter was a specimen.

The reception of the report both by the Legislature and the profession was more favorable than the Revisers had dared to anticipate.

As an indication of this Mr. Duer writes on March 30, 1826, that Peter W. Radcliff, an old New York lawyer, "has taken occasion to express to me in strong terms, his approbation of our plan and proceedings. From him this was unexpected and gratifying. I thought him a stickler for the black-letter school."

That the utmost pains had been taken in the preparation of the initial Chapters is evident from the correspondence. The freest criticism was interchanged between the Revisers. In one of the Albany letters the writer says: "The general method suggested last Spring, was probably right in principle but in detail exceedingly defective. Perfect method is probably unattainable and I am inclined to think with you that we shall find it necessary, as well for this as on other accounts, to retain the work until the whole is completed. * * You cannot treat of any science, even in the most familiar manner, without employing at the very outset, terms of art, a full knowledge of which can only be obtained by referring to subsequent parts of the work, perhaps not until the whole science be mastered." The writer goes on to say that he has taken up the Chapter relating to the duties of towns and counties (Chapter XI), and the subject of taxes and assessments, and while admitting the great difficulty of the task, declares his intention of proceeding according to the original design in the effort to bring order out of the existing confused and complicated mass of the Statutes.

Stimulated, perhaps, by the reception accorded to their labors, the Revisers took heart to proceed. Mr. Wheaton was, however, engrossed with his duties as Reporter and in the completion of his volume of Reports, and Mr. Duer was taken up with his professional engagements in New York. He writes on June 10, 1826, to Mr. Butler, stating these interruptions, and closes by saying: "I am resolved to be proud of your labors, as I cannot exult in my own. The truth is (and we both agree), that you are worth a dozen of such lazy fellows as Wheaton and myself."

At the re-assembling of the Legislature in January, 1827, the Revisers reported Chapters I, II and III. Also Chapter IV (substituted for the chapter of that number as originally proposed), containing a re-enactment of the Bill of Rights of 1787, which, they say, ought to have a permanent place in the statute book, and on January 30, 1827, they presented Chapter V "Of the Civil officers of the State" followed in rapid succession by Chapters VI, VII, VIII, IX, X, XI and XIX. Chapter IX and Chapter XIX related to the whole financial department of the State government. In relation to Chapters V and VI Mr. Butler writes to Mr. Duer: "I send you Chapters V and VI, which were prepared sometime ago, though not copied till lately. In framing the former, you will see that I have drawn liberally on the powers conferred on us and I have added many new provisions." He adds, "I propose next to take up the Highway Acts. I can labor on them without interfering with you or Wheaton."

By this time the work had advanced sufficiently to attract a general interest and to excite the Legislature to effective co-operation. An extra session for the purpose of considering the Revised Statutes was resolved upon and the Legislature adjourned on April 17, 1827, to the second Tuesday of the following September.

Meanwhile, in March, 1827, Mr. Wheaton had resigned and Mr. Spencer had been appointed, April 21, 1827, to fill the vacancy, and had at once engaged in the work and taken an active part in the preparation of Chapter IX.

JOHN C. SPENCER, who now became identified with the revision, had enjoyed advantages of early education superior to those of either of his associates. He was born at Hudson, Columbia County, N. Y., January 6, 1788. His father, Ambrose Spencer, was Attorney General of this State from 1802 to 1804, a Justice of the Supreme Court from 1804 to 1819 and its Chief Justice from 1819 to 1823. The son was trained from boyhood for the Bar, and after graduating at Union College with distinction, pursued his law studies in his father's office. During the administration of Governor Tompkins he was his private secretary, a position which gave him an early practical acquaintance with the routine of work in the Executive Department, and great familiarity with legislative proceedings. He was admitted to the Bar at the age of 23, and shortly afterwards removed from Albany to Canandaigua, then a remote village in a new region of the State. Here he soon became both a political and a professional leader. His bold and vigorous advocacy of the policy and measures of Madison, which preceded the war with Great Britain of 1812, made him conspicuous among the supporters of the President and of Tompkins, the war Governor of that day, but after peace was restored, in the succeeding changes of party relations, he became an ally and friend of DeWitt Clinton. By him he was appointed in 1815 District Attorney for the District embracing the five western counties of the State, and while holding this office was elected as a representative in the fifteenth Congress, in which he was an active member. His term as representative was signalized by his work as chairman of the commission to investigate the United States Bank; he prepared the adverse report as to the Bank, which was the result of the labors of the commission, and which preceded by fifteen years the final onslaught against the same corporation under the administration of General Jackson.

In 1820 he was elected a member of the State Legislature, and served as Speaker of the Assembly, to which body he was again returned the following year, but as a member of the minority. In 1824 he was elected to the State Senate and thus became a member of the Court for the Correction of Errors. During his term as Senator, as Chairman of the Committee on Literature and Education, he made an elaborate and masterly report on the Common School system and the whole subject of education as connected with the State. Thoroughly furnished with this varied equipment, Mr. Spencer brought to the work of the Revision the qualifications which fitted him to supplement, with the greatest efficiency, the efforts of his colleagues. He was an indefatigable worker, of great power of endurance and matchless assiduity in details. He engaged in the Revision with characteristic ardor and readily assumed a large share of the labor which it imposed.

During the interval between the adjournment of the regular session and the opening of the extra session of 1827, much progress was made.

Mr. Duer seems to have determined to clear himself from his own imputation of laziness and on May 19th, writes, "I am at work, as the boys say, in real earnest." "I found," he continues, "that, make what resolution I would, so long as I continued to attend the office, I could do nothing effectual. My time was not in my own power. I therefore concluded to shut myself up at home, and have found the course so profitable, that I shall continue to pursue it. * * I have finished the Canal Laws. They comprise in nine articles about two hundred sections. * * I have received Spencer's analysis of the Second Part but have not yet had leisure to consider it as it must be considered. Upon a cursory inspection, the general arrangement appears to me excellent, but the subdivision of chapters far too numerous." Then he says, "I am satisfied that we shall have to work, each of us, on an average eight or ten hours a day, to enable us to complete our work. It is impossible that Spencer should do all we have allotted to him, and we must endeavor to have the first part completed before the adjournment of the Court of Errors, if possible, by its meeting, and then assist him in completing the second. In the meantime, I take upon myself the chapters of Public Health, of Incorporations, of Trusts, &c."

On June 1, 1827, he writes : "I have continued to work very assiduously, of which you will receive as a sufficient proof that, in three days, I have completed the chapter of Public Health, with the exception of a few penalties that remain to be added. It is completely a new law, as well in language as in arrangement. Before I send it to you I shall submit it to the Health Commissioners for examination."

In reply to this is a letter dated Albany, June 2d, 1827, containing these cheering words :

"I rejoice in your successful exertions, and feel assured that all will go well. Spencer is vigorously engaged. I have received two letters from him this week, the last to-day. In it he sends me Chapter III of Dower. It is well done, so well that he feels proud of it, and wishes us to examine it immediately, with the view of presenting it to Chancellor Kent. He thinks the Chancellor's approbation worth obtaining, and what is, perhaps, a little enthusiastic, he cannot doubt as to securing it by this chapter. Spencer is evidently heart and soul in the work and will give us all the aid we expected from him."

Mr. Spencer's letter refers to the apprehensions of some members of the profession which have been excited "from various causes, some unworthy, and others entitled to consideration. Among them is Chancellor Kent. I want to satisfy him, and at the same time commit him to an approbation of our plan. With this in view I have had an entire copy made of the chapter that I have revised and prepared of Dower, which I propose submitting to him in manuscript for his advice and opinion. * * It is very possible that like all authors, I have mistaken the nature of this particular chapter, but if I do not deceive myself, it is not discreditable. I am hard at work on the statutes of frauds, 13 and 27 Eliz., and 39 and 4 W. and M. I shall *conquer* them."

In reply to this, Mr. Butler writes :

" I agree that the good opinion of Chancellor Kent would be of the greatest service, and without intending an idle compliment, I do verily believe that if anything could remove the prejudice with which he is said to regard our labors, your consolidation of the law of Dower would effect that end. After what I have said you may think I do injustice to Chancellor Kent, when I add that I have no confidence in the success of the proposed reference to him. The grounds of his distrust it would take me too long to explain in writing. *Dies indicabit.*"

In one of Mr. Duer's letters, in the summer of 1827, he speaks of the encouragement he had received from a visit to his office by Thomas Addis Emmet, then the brilliant and accomplished leader of the New York Bar, who was in full sympathy with the work of the Revisers, and who came to Mr. Duer to fulfil a promise to give him in writing, some suggestions touching the law of Descents. This visit occurred only a short time before Mr. Emmet's sudden death, November 14, 1827, in Court during the trial of the cause in which was involved the title to the lands of the Sailor's Snug Harbor. Mr. Van Buren, in his autobiography, a work as yet unpublished, gives a graphic description of Mr. Emmet's death, of which he was an eye-witness :

" In the fall of the year Thomas Addis Emmet was seized with paralysis whilst engaged in the trial of a cause, and died almost immediately. I was one of the opposing counsel in the cause, and as the Court adjourned on the preceding day he expressed to me his surprise that we had kept our suit, the claim of Bishop Inglis of Nova Scotia to the immense estate called the Sailor's Snug Harbor, on foot so long; but added that we could not prolong its life beyond twelve o'clock of the next day. When that time arrived, I followed him from the Bar to the stove, whither he had been called by an acquaintance, and said, 'Well, Mr. Emmet, the hour has come, and we are alive yet!' 'Yes,' he answered, 'but you cannot live much longer!' Immediately after my return to my seat David B. Ogden said to me, 'Look at Emmet! He is going to have a fit!' I looked and replied that it was a mistake. In a few minutes he repeated the alarm more emphatically. I went to Chief-Justice Thompson, before whom the cause was tried, and informed him of Mr. Ogden's suspicions. The Judge observed Mr. E. closely, and replied pleasantly, 'No! no! Ogden is mistaken, his underlip hangs a little lower than usual, but that is natural to him when he is writing!' At that instant, and as I turned towards my seat I saw Mr. Emmet reel in his chair, and extend his hand towards a neighboring pillar. I endeavored to intercept his fall, but without success; he was carried to his house, and died in a few hours."

Mr. Duer had a lively sense of the necessity of leaving the Legislature as little to do as possible in the task of considering the Revision.

He writes June 6, 1827, as to the importance of printing at the head of every new chapter an analysis with references to the former statutes; "We cannot do too much to facilitate the examination of the members. Their gratitude will be exactly in proportion to the extent of the labor from which we relieve them, and we shall relieve ourselves from a multitude of objections, such as Brown of Chautauqua made to the chapter of the Militia."

In a later letter Mr. Duer reports as to the Chapter on Descents, apparently drawn by his Albany colleague, and closes with an expression of personal feeling, which may serve to exhibit the relations which had grown up, in the course of their labors, between the Revisers: "This letter, which I close with reluctance, is intended, of course, for Mr. Spencer as well as yourself. I do trust that our mutual labors have laid the foundation of a friendship which is to cheer and console us during life. It will not be in vain that we have passed together so many useful, virtuous and happy hours. We have learned a good deal of our own hearts and of the characters of each other. We have been taught to bear and forbear under very trying circumstances, and have found that the jealousies and irritations of the hour passed away and our mutual confidence and regard became more solid and permanent. Let us continue to be just to each other and true to ourselves and the triple cord that we have twisted will not soon be broken.''

The extra Session of the Legislature convened September 11, 1827, and as declared by the resolution appointing it, was held for the sole and only purpose of examining and re-enacting the Revision of the Statute Laws of this State. On the first day of the session the Revisers submitted the whole of the First Part in twenty chapters and during the session these and also all the chapters of the Second Part, except Chapter I, were presented and acted upon.

The Legislature adopt elaborate joint rules under which the different chapters were referred to joint committees of the two houses, before whom the Revisers were to attend to assist them in their deliberations; the chapters as reported from the committees were considered by each house and after being passed upon, were referred again to the Revisers for their examination, with power to propose amendments, and under this systematic plan the examination of the work proceeded in the committees and in the two houses, with regularity and ease. The most painstaking scrutiny was exercised and the Revisers were enabled by their final supervision, to guard against injudicious alteration by the many amendments proposed in the committees. Their recommendations as they say in the Introduction to the Second Edition ''were almost always adopted and in general without discussion.''

The session lasted from September 12, 1827, to December 4, 1827, fifty-three days.

It was characterized, say the Revisers, "by patient research and untiring industry on the part of the members" and resulted in the enactment of the entire First and Second Parts of the Revised Statutes except Chapter I of the Second Part, which was laid over until the next meeting of the Legislature.

It was in the Second Part of the proposed system of Administrative Law and especially in the First Chapter, thus postponed by the Legislature, that the Revisers brought the law-making power face to face with the real substance of the reform they proposed.

The First Part dealt with the territorial limits and divisions, the civil polity and internal administration of the State and was concerned with the affairs of municipalities, the regulation of incorporations and of trade, and of the internal police, creating a system which representatives of the people could well understand, with the rudiments of which they were familiar and which, when placed before them in an orderly and perspicuous arrangement, at once attracted their concurrence and acquiescence.

The Second Part brought them into the intricacies of the law relating to the rights of property, real and personal, their acquisition, descent, enjoyment and transmission, reaching to the root and central stem of the entangled growth of the unwritten law of tenures, uses, trusts and devises. The complexity of the law of real estate, the outcome of the feudal system of tenures gave rise, as Blackstone had said, "to the subtelties and refinements into which, in the course of centuries, they were spun out and subdivided."

The lawyers and judges of England united in perpetuating rules and enforcing methods as to the title to land which it became almost impossible to apply with any certainty or safety. The evil became so oppressive that in respect to this branch of the law, as well as to other branches, the cry for reform had gone up from the ranks of the profession itself.

The obscurity of titles, the great hazard and expense of alienation, the frequent and ruinous litigation in which estates were involved, led to those efforts in Parliament in which Brougham and his associates strove with only partial success to attack the abuses of the feudal system as perpetuated by the Courts in England. Even to clear and honest minds this task seemed almost too formidable. The vast political considerations it involved, were too momentous. The change of the law of real estate meant the disturbance of the whole framework of society.

Meanwhile, the law of real property described by Mr. Cruise, one of its most learned commentators, "as the most extensive and abstruse branch of English jurisprudence," remained, as the Revisers say, "very imperfectly understood by any of the legal profession who have not made it an object of peculiar study and attention, and so remote are its principles and maxims from ordinary apprehension, that to the mass of the community they seem to be shrouded in impenetrable mystery."

This whole vast subject, including the law of estates in expectancy, of remainders vested and contingent, of uses and trusts, formal, active and passive, of forfeitures, fines and recovery, of powers appendant and appurtenant, collateral or in gross, was enshrined with its cabalistic terms and its ensnaring devices in the chaotic mass of the unwritten Common Law, the undefined powers of Chancery, the dicta of judges, and Acts of Parliament, which as interpreted in Westminster Hall, served only to make the confusion in which the system was involved worse confounded.

While English Courts were struggling in the network of legal fictions and devices by which the law of the kingdom was to retain the enslaving impress of the feudal system, long after the people had broken down all its other barriers, the Revisers believed that the hindrances to the work of reform in the mother country had no place here.

True, the whole law of real estate had been, as far as

possible, transferred to this side of the ocean and was being administered in our Courts by men who delighted in its subtleties and fictions, but the Revisers were bold enough to strike out measures of reform by which, while retaining all that was really serviceable in the existing system, they might break away, once and forever, from the bondage of a barbarous age perpetuated by generations of black-letter judges.

"Our law of real estate" they say "is not an uniform and consistent system, complex only from the multitude of its rules and the variety of its details; but it embraces two sets of distinct and opposite maxims, different in origin and hostile in principle. We have first, the rules of the common law connected throughout with the doctrine of tenures, and meant and adapted to maintain the feudal system in all its rigor; and we have next, an elaborate system of expedients, very artificial and ingenious, devised in the course of ages by courts and lawyers, with some aid from the legislature, for the express purpose of evading the rules of the Common Law, both in respect to the qualities and the alienation of estates, and to introduce modifications of property before prohibited or unknown. It is the conflict continued through centuries between these hostile systems that has generated that infinity of subtleties and refinements with which this branch of our jurisprudence is overloaded."

They laid the axe to the root of the tree of feudal tenures and feudal restrictions. The keynote of their reform was struck in these plain declarations, which, simple and necessary as they seem to us, were a new language in the ears of many of their generation, who were accustomed only to receive what had been said by them of old time.

"The interests of society require that the power of the owner to fetter the alienation and suspend the ownership of an estate by future limitations should be confined within certain limits;" and, after stating the evils and abuses incident to the existing law, they add: "The remedy seems to the Revisers obvious and effectual: it is to abolish all technical rules and distinctions, having no relation to the essential nature of property and the means of its beneficial enjoyment, but which, derived from the feudal system, rest solely upon feudal reasons. * * The principles by which they have been governed in proposing alterations, may be very briefly stated. If a rule of law is just and wise in itself, apply it universally as far as the reasons upon which it is founded extend, and in no instance permit it to be evaded ; if it is irrational and foolish, or the reasons upon which it is rested are obsolete, abolish it at once."

They point out, in later sentences, that their proposed provisions, if adopted, " will sweep away an immense mass of useless refinements and distinctions ; will relieve the law of real property to a great extent from its abstruseness and uncertainty, and render it, as a system, intelligible and consistent." "In England," they further say "the continuance of the landed property in the hands of the aristocracy is the basis upon which the monarchy itself may be said to rest, but, with us, it should never be forgotten that it is the partibility, the frequent division and unchecked alienation of property, that are essential to the health and vigor of our republican institutions."

It is impossible for me to go into details, either as to the evils and abuses which the Revisers undertook to cure by their new system of written rules governing this entire field of the law as well as its cognate branches, dealt with in the second part of the Revised Statutes, or as to the character and reasons of the radical and far-reaching remedies they created. The student of our law, who would acquaint himself with these particulars, must find them in the volumes of the reports of the Revisers, in which are displayed a wealth of learning, of research, of careful analysis and discrimination, of painstaking and conscientious application of the true principles of law and justice to the rights of the people. It is in these reports, and especially in the notes accompanying the statutes as first reported, that the work of the Revision is to be seen in an interior light which reveals the marvelous industry and minute care bestowed upon it. Probably, very few members of our profession have ever had the time, or the inclination, or even the occasion, to pursue this study, and I presume there are not many copies of these reports extant, but they embody a whole commentary on the then existing state of the law.

The first edition of the Revised Statutes did not contain the Reports or the notes which accompanied them.

" In these notes," says Judge Edmunds in his edition of the Revised Statutes of 1863, "the profession have felt that they have often found, in the language of Lord Coke, the very lock and key to set open the windows of the Statutes." They were published in the second edition, and will there be found, as well as in Judge Edmunds' later edition, a lasting monument to the research and learning of their authors.

Nor is it necessary to enquire into the wisdom of the system of the laws of real estate, which the Revisers proposed and secured. They had to grapple with difficulties which were inherent in the subject, and which they were required to solve, so as to disturb as little as possible the real foundations of the law as a necessary bulwark of society ; they had to devise new methods, without destroying established rights ; they had to keep the *via media* between old abuses and doubtful innovations. It is enough to say that the system they devised has stood the test of time, and remains as little changed as any part of their work, and as little needing change. Perhaps they might have gone further in the direction of reform, but it must be remembered that the changes they proposed are to be viewed in the light of the time in which they lived, sixty years ago, before a railroad had been laid in this hemisphere, and when the arts and appliances of modern civilization were in their infancy. It has been well said that " it is the creative part of the reformer's work which at once shows his skill and produces real fruit. It is the sagacity to devise the scheme of amendment, it is the patience to prosecute it, the caution, the conciliation, the dexterity, the unwearied perseverance to carry it through all difficulties to a practical consummation ; these are the qualities wanted for the safe and judicious reform of the law."

The extra session of 1827 settled the question of the acceptability of the general plan of the Revision. No step backward was now to be feared. The interval between the adjournment of the Legislature, December 4, 1827, and its re-assembling for the regular session in January, 1828, was occupied by the Revisers in preparation for the task of carrying through the Legislature the more important and novel portions of their work to which I have referred.

Their next step forward brought the Revisers themselves into the sphere of legislation, where, by their voices and their votes they were able to aid in perfecting the reforms they recommended. Mr. Spencer was elected to the Legislature of 1828, as a Senator from the Seventh District, and Mr. Butler as a Member of the Assembly from Albany. Party politics ran high, as always in the Assembly District which includes the State Capital, and the local influences were adverse at the time to the opponents of Governor Clinton, among whom, as a member of the Democratic-Republican party, Mr. Butler was classed ; but it is a striking proof of the popular interest which had been created in the work of the Revision, that the political leaders recognized the importance of aiding the work by the election of one of the Revisers. Mr. Hammond, in his somewhat desultory but entertaining Political History of New York, says :

"There is no doubt a majority of the electors in Albany were opposed to General Jackson and his party. But I presume many of the electors voted for Mr. Butler, who were against Jackson, because it was known that the Revised Statutes would be acted upon by the Assembly then to be chosen, and that the services of Mr. Butler would be highly beneficial to the public upon that occasion. I was myself warmly opposed to the Jackson party, and yet voted for Mr. Butler, for the reason I have stated."

On the floor of the Senate and the Assembly of 1828, the two Revisers were able to maintain and advance their scheme of reform with the great advantage of their thorough knowledge of the subject and their high forensic abilities. They had to meet all objections urged by members of their own profession who were fellow-members with them in the Legislature, and to defend themselves against the charge of innovation raised here, as in England, by the whole body of old-fashioned lawyers who dreaded change and clung to precedent. In the Assembly Mr. Butler during the regular and extra sessions, made not less than five hundred or six hundred speeches on the separate sections proposed, and in both Houses the result of the discussions was the entire success of the Revision.

It was during the session of 1828 and on February 11th of that year, that DeWitt Clinton, then Governor of the State, died suddenly at Albany, ending a great career and leaving an enduring fame. The presence in the Assembly, as a representative from the Capital, of one of the Revisers, gave him the opportunity of advocating in the Legislature a generous measure on behalf of the family of Governor Clinton, which was all the more appreciated from the fact that it was promoted by a political opponent. The measure, however, failed for want of a two-thirds vote.

The session closed with the work of the Revision still unfinished, and again an extra session was found necessary. It was appointed for September 9, 1828.

During the recess the whole energies of the Revisers were bent to the completion of the work. Mr. Duer undertook the final Revision and perfecting of the troublesome first Chapter of Part II, and devoted himself exclusively for six weeks to this delicate task. The severity of the labor, the pressure of his professional duties in the office of United States District Attorney, to which he had been appointed in 1827, by President Adams, and perhaps the fact that their position as members of the Legislature and given his associates superior facilities in the prosecution of the work, led to the withdrawal of Mr. Duer from further active participation in it. He had no share in the preparation of the Third or Fourth Parts, and I gather from the documents and reports that with the exception of assisting in the preparation of the First Chapter of Part II he did no more than to give occasional advice upon some of the provisions of the succeeding chapters.

Mr. Duer's share in the work was thus, as we have seen, specially in the preparation of some of the Chapters of Part I, particularly those relating to Elections, the Public Health and of Incorporations and on Weights and Measures, and in the First Chapter of the Second Part. The other Chapters of the First Part were either the exclusive work of Mr. Butler or were in the first instance prepared by him and submitted to Mr. Duer and to Mr. Wheaton, so long as he was a member of the body, for their Revision. Mr. Spencer had a share in preparing some of the Chapters of the First Part, especially Chapter IX, relating to the Finances of the State, and all of the Second Part except Chapter I, and all the Third and Fourth Parts were the joint work of himself and Mr. Butler. It is impossible to state with absolute accuracy, by whom the different Chapters of the Third and Fourth Parts were originally prepared.

Mr. Duer having retired, the remaining Revisers divided the work between themselves, and were in constant and joint labor, chiefly at Albany. Each of them had held the office of District Attorney, and thus were able to co-operate intelligently in the preparation of the Fourth Part, relating to Crimes and their Punishment, but I believe that the main work in the preparation of that part, devolved on Mr. Spencer, while a great portion of the Third Part relating to Courts of Justice, suits and proceedings, were the work of his colleague.

In the notes to the Fourth Part are many interesting details in reference to the English Criminal Law and to those statutes " written in blood," which inflicted inhuman penalties for comparatively venial offences.

The radical changes made by the Revisers were a step

forward, but not too far, in the interests of humanity as well as of justice.

Some of their recommendations as to crimes and their punishment were not adopted by the Legislature. Among them is a proposed section, imposing upon any landlord letting houses for disorderly purposes, a liability as aider and abettor in the unlawful acts of the tenant, which anticipated some provisions subsequently put upon the statute book, as a means of resistance to the aggressions of the forces arrayed against social order.

The Revisers' note which failed to impress the Legislature of 1827 seems to me inspired by good sense as well as sound morals.

"If there is any utility whatever in the laws against disorderly houses, they should be made effectual against those who afford the means of violating them. So long as owners of houses shall be permitted to lease them at extravagant rents enhanced by the fact that they are to be used for the worst purposes, the laws against such violations of public decency will be ineffectual. * * It is believed that the proposed provision will be more effectual than any existing law."

The work at Albany, both before and after Mr. Duer's withdrawal, was done in the office of the resident Reviser, No. 109 State street. Mr. Andrew J. Colvin, one of the oldest members of our Bar, and who has served the State as a Senator, was at that time a student at law in the office. He has given me some interesting reminiscences of the work.

He says :

"In answer to your inquiry I would say, that in the Revision of the statutes a great deal of the work was done by your father, and John Duer, afterwards Judge of the Superior Court of New York, in the basement office of the house in which you lived. There your father worked and wrote, early and late, as did Mr. Duer also ; my recollection is that the whole revision in regard to uses and trusts and powers was prepared by Mr. Duer ; then copied by me, for I copied a considerable part of the Revision, and that these subjects were then taken up by your father, and by him revised and corrected. They were then discussed and further amended, and finally copied for the printer. Mr. Duer wrote a shocking hand, and I could make little out of his scrawlings, unless aided by him or your father.

Your father and John C. Spencer, I think, prepared the entire work on practice, pleadings and criminal law. That portion of it relating to the civil divisions of the State and kindred subjects, such as Boards of Supervisors and Courts of limited jurisdiction, was almost entirely prepared by your father, if my memory is not at fault.

I was a student in your father's office for about five years.

After the Revision was fully under way, your father gave almost his whole time to it, and as I was with him early and late, I saw a great deal of him, and learned not only to respect, but to love him. He never spoke to me an unkind word during the whole time I was a student with him. He was one of the most amiable and excellent of men, kind-hearted, gentle and tender; and yet a man of great capacity and learning, with industry irrepressible, and with a patience in going to the bottom of any point or matter that he was studying, which was untiring.

To me he was a model man, and since we separated, I do not think a day has passed in which I have not thought of him, and blessed God that the tender, forming years of my life were brought within the influences of his noble precepts and example."

The extra session of 1828 convened September 9, 1828, and terminated December 10, 1828. Like the former extra session, it was devoted exclusively to the consideration of the Revision, and the presence of the Revisers, made the work thorough and satisfactory.

In one important particular, the Revisers received most important aid from the Legislature, who, as will be seen, had been educated to a point of reform, at which they took an advance step beyond the proposals of the Revisers and became wiser than their teachers.

In no department of the law did fiction hold more undisputed sway than, in suits between contesting claimants to land.

By the common law, land could pass only by actual

change of seisin and possession on the soil. Every transfer of land was required to be open and notorious.

To avoid the inconvenience which this arbitrary rule created, instead of resorting to the power of Parliament to enact a simple mode of land transfers and of determining disputes about land, the lawyers and judges invented, in the action of ejectment, the most intricate and complex of all the fictions in which the genius of the common law delights.

Sergeant Warren, in "Ten Thousand a Year," has given a graphic description of this form of action, which he says dates from the close of Edward II. or beginning of Edward III. (A. D. 1327). He explains how it is that when one honest Briton claims a parcel of land of which another honest Briton is in possession, instead of the two parties impleading each other, as in any other action to recover money or property, they are obliged to set up a couple of puppets, John Doe and Richard Roe by name, who fall upon one another in a very quaint fashion, after the manner of Punch and Judy. John Doe pretends to be the real plaintiff, and Richard Roe the real defendant. John Doe says that the land which Richard Roe has is his, because one Jones gave him a lease of it, and that he came on the premises where he was met by Richard Roe, who ousted him and thus became what was termed in the lingo of the law the "casual ejector."

The attorney for John Doe, the fictitious plaintiff, annexed to his declaration a notice from Richard Roe, the "casual ejector," to the party really in possesion, notifying him to appear within a limited time and defend the suit, or in default of such appearance judgment will go against the casual ejector and the real tenant be turned out of possession. Thereupon the real tenant comes into Court by his attorney and admits as true the whole fictitious narrative of the declaration, denying only the superior title of the real claimant.

When the question of fact was thus in a condition to be tried, the whole frame work of fiction disappeared, having served its turn to bring the parties into Court. All this, as the little Marchioness in "Old Curiosity Shop" would say, "was making believe very much," but it was a clumsy sort of contrivance which suited the Anglo-Saxon temperament, and which was enshrined as carefully in the Common Law system of the State of New York, as if it had been the corner-stone of the whole fabric.

This rubbish of fiction, the Revisers proposed utterly to abolish and destroy. They say in their report on this subject, that they had received many applications to do away with these absurd methods, and they took the initiative in discarding this particular absurdity. But in respect to another and older method of asserting right to land and compelling a trial of the title, known as "Fine and Recovery," dating back beyond the Conquest and adopted in this State from its earliest settlement, they seem to have thought it too deeply rooted in the soil of real estate tenures to warrant its disturbance, and so they only proposed to modify it.

A "fine" meant in the jargon of the ancient law not, as now understood, a penalty, but a feoffment (*i. e.* a deed) upon record, so called because it put an end (*finis*) to litigation ; and what was called "levying a fine" was a formal proceeding by which a person claiming title to land took visible possession of it under his claim, made proclamation in open court at four successive terms, advertised in an official paper for a certain time, posted a notice on the Court House door, and placed a deed to somebody on record, which being done, unless the party in possession brought an action within five years after the fine was so levied, his title was barred.

The Revisers retained this ancient mode of procedure with various simplifications, but also reported several entirely new provisions which were so framed, that they might be taken as substitutes for fines and common recoveries. When these titles were taken up in the Assembly, that body not only approved the views of the Revisers in general, but carried them to a still greater extent, and on September 18, 1828, passed a resolution directing the Revisers to report the titles so as to abolish fines and recoveries, to simplify the action of ejectment and other proceedings to compel the determination of claims to real property, and, upon this being done, the Legislature adopted them, and by section 24 of Title 7 of Chapter 4 of Part III of the Revised Statutes it was declared "that all writs of rights, writs of dower, writs of entry and writs of assize, all fines and common recoveries, and all other real actions known to the Common Law, not enumerated and retained in this chapter ; and all writs and other process heretofore used in real action, which are not specially retained in this chapter, shall be and they are hereby abolished."

And thus it came to pass that fines and recoveries, as the Court of Appeals say in McGregor *vs.* Comstock, 17 N. Y., 162, were "with other antiquities abolished and a simpler system substituted."

It was not until three years later, and after the Revised Statutes had gone into full operation and shown the action of ejectment stripped of its feudal trappings, that England, following the lead of New York, enacted by 3 and 4 William IV., c. 74, that no fine or recovery should be levied or suffered after December 31, 1833. But in respect to the action of ejectment the good example of New York bore no fruit in the native soil of John Doe and Richard Roe, until the fifteenth year of Queen Victoria, when by the Practice Act of 1853 they were legislated out of existence as parties in ejectment.

The extra Session of 1828 ended December 10, having occupied ninety-one days, during which the Legislature and the Revisers accomplished the design of completing their joint work before the end of the year. The entire body of the Revised Statutes was adopted December 10, 1828. Those portions which had been enacted at previous sessions and which had already taken effect and gone into operation, consisting of Chapers VI, VIII, IX, X, XIII and XIV, Title II of Chapters XV, and Chapters XVI and XVIII of Part First, which took effect January 1, 1828, and

Chapter XVII of Part First, which took effect May 1, 1828, were declared to have taken effect at those dates respectively, and the remaining chapters were directed "to commence and take effect as laws on the first day of January, 1830." The publication of the entire Revised Statutes in three volumes was committed by the Legislature to the Revisers with very ample powers of alteration to conform the statutes to any changes which might be made by the Legislature after their passage and before the final publication. They were authorized to certify, by any two of their number, to the correctness of the printed statutes.

The original text of the entire Revised Statutes, supplemented by the Act of December 10, 1828, above referred to, is contained in a folio volume printed for the Legislature of 1828, by Packard & Van Benthuysen. It is a noble specimen of the typographical art, almost rivalling the famous classics of Baskerville. A few copies are extant. One of them, a gift of our learned associate, Judge Edmonds, is in the library of the Association.

The several volumes were issued as soon as completed ; the official certificate prefixed to the first volume bears date January 31, 1829, that prefixed to the second volume, June 5, 1829, and that prefixed to the third volume, September 10, 1830.

The whole work of preparing the three volumes of the Revised Statutes for publication with the marginal notes and references, and the index, which, as originally published, was a model of accuracy and completeness, was done by Mr. Butler and Mr. Spencer. It involved immense labor, and the closest application, as they were under an absolute responsibility for accuracy to the Legislature and the public, and well knew that the whole profession would scrutinize the work with jealous care. The untiring and indefatigable industry of Mr. Spencer in scrutinizing every line and word and letter of the text and of the index is shown by his many letters, which are marvels of neatness, precision and exactitude, alike in their delicate chirography and in their minuteness and of detail. A corres-

ponding fidelity in regard to every item of the complicated work was shown by his colleague.

The copyright of the Revised Statutes was the property
of the State of New York, and was taken out in the name
of Azariah C. Flagg, Secretary of State, in trust, for the
benefit of the People of the State of New York.

This applied, however, only to the first edition, the subsequent editions, including the second and third, which
were published by the Revisers, were private undertakings,
an Act of the Legislature, passed in 1830, having provided
that any person might publish the Revised Statutes, and
that the work so published might be read in evidence if
accompanied with a certificate of the Secretary of State, or
two of the Revisers, but all editions are required to be
paged in conformity to the first edition.

To judges and lawyers unaccustomed to Codes, the appearance of the Revised Statutes was an event of the first
magnitude.

It came upon the profession at a time when the earlier
agitation of questions of reform in England had demon-
strated the need of change and improvement, without introducing any new methods to supersede old abuses.

The fact that a whole system, embracing almost all the
projected reforms about which English jurists were debat-
ing, had come into being, with the absolute force of law,
was almost a surprise, notwithstanding the years of preparatory work during which it had been carried on.

The Revisers had done their part in creating a sound
public opinion in favor of their work, by publishing
in advance the main portions of the new Statutes.   Mr.
Spencer, with his accustomed industry, had in a series of
articles in the *Ontario Messenger*, the local journal of his
district, given an outline of the proposed changes in the
Statutes, and by this and other publications, the profession
had been advised of the leading features of the work.

In the main the judges and the lawyers accepted the
new system with favor.   But, as always, when changes are

inaugurated, some doubted. Judge Roosevelt, to whom I have already referred, told me that the old lawyers would not examine the new Statutes with sufficient care to note the alterations they made, and most of them took counsel of their prejudices. As an instance, he related an incident, which I give, in substance, in his own words. An old citizen of New York, named Boardman, who lived on Broadway, next door but one above Park Place, by his last will and testament devised certain real estate to a son, giving him an estate for life with remainder to his heirs. The will was made before the Revised Statutes took effect; the testator died after they took effect; the devisee submitted the will to Peter A. Jay for his opinion as to the estate devised.

Meeting Mr. Jay, and knowing that the will had been submitted to him, Roosevelt asked him if he had given his opinion. "Yes," said he. "And did you give an opinion that the son took an estate in fee?" "Certainly; why not, under the rule in Shelley's case?" "But," said Roosevelt, "the Revised Statutes have changed all that, and abolished the rule in Shelley's case." "What have the Revised Statutes got to do with a will made before they took effect?" was Mr. Jay's rejoinder, to which Roosevelt said: "If you will look at Section Twenty-eight of the first Chapter of Part Two, you will see that it applies to this will." Mr. Jay went and looked, and found a plain provision changing the English judicial rule of construction, which had been in force ever since the twenty-first year of the reign of Queen Elizabeth.

Shelley's case grew out of a family quarrel over an inheritance in which Queen Elizabeth so far intermeddled in her capacity of the "Fountain of all Justice and Life of the Law," as Lord Coke describes her, on the pretext of preventing, as he further says, "long, tedious and chargeable suits between parties near in blood and gentlemen of good and ancient family," as to summon all the Justices of England of the Courts of Queens Bench and the Common Pleas and the Barons of the Exchequer to resolve the question in dispute. This was, simply, whether the estate in certain lands of Edward Shelley, the common ancestor, and his wife Joan, vested in them with remainder limited to their heirs, was a life estate or a fee. One branch of the Shelley family claimed under a deed made by Edward Shelley after his wife's death, and the other branch claimed by descent from the same Edward, whose deed they sought to avoid because, as they claimed, he took only a life estate.

After argument and reargument, judgment was finally given, that Edward Shelley and his wife, Joan, took an estate in fee, and the rule which thus passed into the jurisprudence of England as the rule in Shelley's case, determined that, however contrary to the intent of the person creating the estate, a grantee or devisee takes the fee even when given with an express limitation in favor of his heirs.

This rule operated very often to defeat the intention of grantors and testators, not by a statute, but by a technical judge-made rule turning on the particular word, " heirs." For if the grant were to a grantee for life, with remainder to his issue, the remainder was good, and he took only a life estate, but if the unlucky testator or grantor, or his conveyancer, used the word " heirs," instead of " issue," he gave a fee. Again, the rule might be evaded by giving an estate for years to the first taker. Thus it was founded on no reason possibly applicable in this State, and yet it had been slavishly followed by our Courts as an integral part of the English Common Law of real property, until swept away by the section to which Mr. Jay was referred by Judge Roosevelt.

It still remains in full force in England, and is there claimed to be binding as a rule of law not dependent on the construction of the grant or will nor the intent of the grantor or testator.

Although the end had thus happily crowned the work, it had not been unattended by the anxieties and discouragements which never fail to visit the path of earnest toilers in unaccustomed fields. The sense of responsibility, the dread of failure, the keen apprehension of unjust criticism, and above all, the fear of coming short of the mark which they had themselves set as the standard of a true performance, gave many anxious and foreboding hours to the Revisers, whose disquieting thoughts are expressed in the correspondence, often revealing the deep despondency and anxiety which overclouded all their anticipations of success.

Time would fail me to point out, in detail, the many improvements in our law which owe their origin wholly to the work of the Revisers.

Enough has been said to illustrate its general method, and to indicate with what caution and wisdom the plan of reproducing whatever in the law of England could be simplified and made to accord with our needs was so pursued as to leaven the old lump of feudalism with the new leaven of democracy.

The Revisers seem to have had in mind, and to have kept in mind, the wise injunction of Burke, that "when the useful parts of an old establishment are kept, and what is superseded is fitted to what is retained, a vigorous mind, steady persevering attention, various powers of comparison and combination, and the resources of an understanding fruitful in expedients, are to be exercised."

With the exception of the Bill of Rights, every section of the entire work was substantially original in the form in which it appears in the Revised Statutes, and it may be claimed for the Revisers that while Blackstone in his Commentaries had presented the great body of the unwritten law of England as an orderly system for the student, and as a guide in the administration of justice, they first gave it form and reality as the supreme rule for every function of the governing power.

No better summary of the plan and the performance of their work, has been given than that contained in the address of William Kent, son of the Chancellor, and for some time a Judge of the Circuit, in this city, in his address at the meeting of the Bar, in memory of his lifelong friend the last survivor of the three co-workers.

Speaking of the Revised Statutes, Judge Kent said :

"You, Mr. Chairman, remember, as I do, the reluctance and apprehension with which those laws were received. All changes in a nation's laws unavoidably produce inconvenience, and familiarity and study are necessary to produce a general acknowledgment of their benefit. This acknowledgment the Revised Statutes have now received from even the seniors of the profession. The principle of the revision was wise and conservative. Acknowledged evils only were removed ; doubts were cleared away ; the doctrines of important decisions were extended ; anomalies were suppressed or reconciled ; but still the essence of the old laws was preserved, and even the habits of the lawyers were wisely respected. The peculiarity of the common law itself appears to have been the guiding rule of the Revisers. and the Statutes were formed, not on the model of an inexorable and abstract system, but in accordance with the customs and wants of the profession and the nation. This code was not the direct and arbitrary statute, going straight to its object, like the cannon ball, shattering what it reaches and shattering that it may reach, but resembled the village road described in the beautiful lines in Wallenstein :

> 'The road the human being travels,
>   That on which Blessing comes and goes, doth follow
> The river's course, the valley's playful windings,
>   Curves round the cornfield and the hill of vines,
> Honoring the holy bounds of property.'

I may be permitted to add what follows :

"I am not able to make partition of merit among the three distinguished men who performed this great legal work. We know that some of the most important chapters were the production of him (Judge Duer), whose exuberant learning and talents received recently a touching and eloquent eulogy from Mr. Butler himself, in this vicinity. All who know the hardy genius and indomitable energy of John C. Spencer, will readily believe that his spirit pervaded the whole work. But judging only from internal evidence, I cannot avoid believing that much of the essential excellence of the Revised Statutes, and more of the labor which adapted them to our general system of jurisprudence, the plan and order of the work, the correctness of its style, the learning of the notes, the marginal references, and the admirable index which accompanied it, should be ascribed to the *limæ labor*, the patient touches of unwearied art, bestowed by the skill and matchless assiduity of Mr. Butler.

Side by side with this tribute let me place another which has come to me, and in which one of our ablest and most experienced jurists, speaking thirty years later than Judge Kent, gives testimony equally clear and emphatic as to the work and its authors.

WASHINGTON, Jan. 17th, 1889.

WM. ALLEN BUTLER, Esq.,

Dear Sir.—I regret not to be able to attend the presentation of the portraits of John Duer, Benjamin F. Butler and John C. Spencer to the Bar Association of New York City, on the 22d instant. I have always had the highest admiration for those able and accomplished jurists, and owe them personally a large debt of gratitude. In 1828, in December, there was a Special Session of the Legislature for considering the amendments which had been proposed to the Revised Statutes. Mr. Spencer had been elected a member of the Senate for the special purpose of explaining these amendments and carrying them through. I resided at that time in my native place, Bern, Albany County, but happened to be spending some weeks in Albany whilst the Legislature was sitting, and attended every day in the gallery to hear the lucid and luminous explanations which Mr. Spencer gave to the various laws. His fluent and accurate speech, and far reaching views made a deep impression upon me and gave me the first stimulus in the direction of legal studies. The work accomplished by the Revisers was not only one of great utility in bringing together and harmonizing the various statutes relating to the same subject, over the whole field of statute law, but it exhibited an analytical symmetry and beauty which are themselves worthy of every student's attention. No better analysis can be framed of the municipal law of a State than that which forms the basis of the Revised Statutes of New York. They are in this, as well as in other respects, worthy to stand by the side of the Revised Statutes of Rome, made under the auspices of Justitian and usually called the Codex or Code, though having no resemblance to what is understood, in modern times, as a Code.

I never had any personal acquaintance with Mr. Spencer, and only knew him as the expounder of the Revised Statutes. With the other Revisers, it was my good fortune to have some personal intercourse, which I highly valued. I had the honor to be associated with your father (Mr. Butler), in 1855, in my first argument before the Supreme Court of the United States, in the great case of Murray's Lessee *vs.* Hoboken Land and Improvement Company, in which the question of due process of law was discussed. Mr. Butler, of course, took the lead and argued the Constitutional question, and argued it with wonderful learning and ability. I can never forget the kindness and considerate attention which I received from him during our conferences on the case. His wealth of learning and the freedom with which he imparted his views to one so much younger than himself won my sincerest regard. Judge Duer I often met at the house of my brother-in-law, Judge Woodruff, his associate on the Bench of the Superior Court. His learning in the law, his various acquirements, his rich discourse and charm of manner, can never be forgotten by those who have had the opportunity of social intercourse with him.

I cannot resist the desire of paying my feeble tribute to the memory of those great men.

Sincerely yours,

JOSEPH P. BRADLEY.

At the time the Revised Statutes, as an active system, went into operation, January 1, 1830, the Supreme Court was composed of Chief Justice Savage and Judges Sutherland and Marcy. The Judges of the eight Circuits were, most of them, men of exceptional ability, whose names are familiar to us—Ogden Edwards, James Emott the elder, James Vanderpoel, Esek Cowen, Nathan Williams, Samuel Nelson, Daniel Moseley and Addison Gardiner. Greene C. Bronson was Attorney-General of the State.

The first mention of the Revised Statutes in the Reports is in the case of Watts *vs.* the Public Administrator, 4 Wendell, 168, involving the validity of the will of John G. Leake, a wealthy bachelor and recluse in the city of New York, and a member of the legal profession, who died in June, 1820, leaving no relatives. A will, in his own handwriting, without date, unsigned and not attested, was found at the bottom of an iron chest. It gave the bulk of his estate to Robert Watts, a son of his friend John Watts, on condition of changing his name to Leake ; in case of his refusal to comply with the condition, or of his dying without issue, the estate was to vest in trustees for the maintenance of an orphan asylum.

This will was void as to the testator's real estate, situated in several interior counties, which escheated to the State, but it was admitted to probate by the Surrogate of New York as a will of personal property.

Chancellor Walworth, on appeal, reversed the Surrogate's decree and ordered letters of administrations to issue to the Public Administrator (1 Paige, 383). The Court of Errors, in turn, reversed the Chancellor by a vote of seventeen to nine (4 Wendell, 168).

In the meantime the Revisers had taken up the subject of wills of personal property, and finding, as they say in their notes, that "the law and practice of the Ecclesiastical Courts have, until a recent period, been hidden mysteries," they placed the execution of wills of real and personal property under the same rule and prescribed a like mode of execution and attestation for both.

England followed this reform by the Statute of Victoria, which took effect in 1838.

When the Leake will case came to the Court of Errors, where, as appears from the original printed brief for the appellants, in my possession, the counsel were John V. Henry, Peter A. Jay and Benjamin F. Butler, opposed by I. Platt and David B. Ogden, the new provisions of the Revised Statutes were in force, and the Reporter contents himself with saying that "although the case was argued by the counsel with more than usual ability, and the opinions of the Judges evince the fullest consideration of the principles of law applicable to the subject, still the Revised Statutes of this State which went into operation on the 1st January, 1830, having placed wills of personal property on the same footing with wills of real estate, this case and the decision of it have become more a matter of curious interest, than of practical use."

The result of the Leake will case was that on the death of Robert Watts, without issue, his father, who was his sole next-of-kin, generously relinquished all right to the estate, and the personal property was applied to the creation of the Leake and Watts Orphan Asylum, a most beneficent institution, which for many years has occupied the commanding site recently purchased for the proposed cathedral of the Protestant Episcopal Church, the Orphan House trustees having selected a more remote suburban property.

The State of New York retains in its Common School fund a sum of at least one hundred thousand dollars, the proceeds of the testator's real estate, as an escheat, one of the grounds on which the Legislature has refused repeated applications for its release in aid of the charity for which it was intended, being that, as Leake was a lawyer, he ought to have known better than to make a void will, thus visiting this sin of a childless testator upon the orphans of other fathers for untold generations.

The first reported case in which the provisions of the Revised Statutes are cited and applied is Curtis *vs.* Staring, 4 Wendell, 198, a question of practice as to the review of a decision by referees. During the same term the new regulations were frequently enforced.

The earliest case of prominent importance involving a construction of provisions of the Revised Statutes introducing radical changes in the law, arose in 1835 in the well known and leading case of Lorillard *vs.* Coster (5th Wendell, 172, 14 Id., 265.)

George Lorillard died in September, 1832, a bachelor, possessed of an estate valued at about $3,000,000, most of which was real property in the city of New York, the annual income being at the time of his death between $80,000 and $100,000. By his will made in October, 1831, after the Revised Statutes had gone into effect, he gave the bulk of his property to his executors, as trustees, for the benefit of twelve nephews and nieces, who were to enjoy the income, and at the expiration of two years after the death of all of them, the estate was to be divided equally among all their children and grandchildren *per stirpes*. The provisions of the will as to the trust thus created, set in motion a protracted controversy as to the intent and effect of the new provisions of the Revised Statutes, in reference to the power of the owners of estates to fetter their alienation and suspend their ownership, and also the provisions by which the statutes sought to reach a modified abolition of uses and trusts.

In this litigation the parties in interest sought the professional services of the Revisers themselves, all of whom were retained in the cause and took part, on different sides, in the argument. The report of the case in the Court of last resort contains, in the opinions of Chief Justice Savage, Judge Nelson and Senators Mason, Young and Tracy, a splendid encomium on the work of the Revisers in this department of the law. The Court unanimously held that the attempted suspension of the alienation of the trust estate during a period of twelve lives, was wholly void as against the provisions of the Revised Statutes, and established the principle which has since been invariably applied, that every testamentary disposition since the Revision took effect must be tested by these provisions. Chief Justice Savage, in the course of his opinion, says:

" It is known to us all, that preparatory to the late Revision of the statutes, the work of revising, analyzing, collating, composing, and, if there were such a word, codifying, and presenting to the Legislature in a new form the statutes of the State, was committed to three gentlemen, distinguished for their legal learning, their ability and their industry. The result of their labors is before us in their report to the Legislature. Whenever their recommendations have been adopted by the Legislature, and their notes have declared the object in view in plain language, free from all technicality, we may safely pursue that object, and in the path pointed out."

He then reviews the observations of the Revisers in their

notes upon the sections applicable to the case, and declares that in their effort " to extricate this branch of the law from the perplexity and obscurity in which it was before involved, they have certainly succeeded to a very great extent if not entirely."

As to uses, trusts and powers characterized by the Revisers as probably the most intricate department in all our jurisprudence, the Chief Justice approves their course when, as he says :

"Instead of endeavoring to unravel the mysteries of uses and trusts, or to cast light into the numerous dark and winding passages of the labyrinth of powers, they demolished the whole. The learned antiquarian will pause and ponder over this vast pile of ruins ; venerable, at least, for their antiquity, the erection of which occupied centuries and put in requisition the labors of kings, ecclesiastics and laymen. Upon these ruins have been erected new edifices—a new system of uses and trusts, apparently plain and intelligible, and adapted to the real wants of society ; but whether it is so in reality is yet to be proved. Instead of the labyrinth of powers, we have a new building of modern architecture, through which I hope we may pass with safety, with such clue as the Revisers have furnished."

Senator Young, after commenting upon the sections in question, says :

" The language of these several sections tend to one simple object—the entire abrogation, the utter repeal of all Common Law tenures, with all their complicated incidents and appurtenances ; and the substitution in their stead of a new tenure, and new trusts, uses and powers adapted to the simplicity of our institutions. The constitution of this State authorizes the abrogation of the Common Law ; and unless this ancient, complicated and barbarous system exercises a power and a thraldom over us, superior to the constitution and laws, it is entirely abrogated in relation to the tenure, the acquisition, the enjoyment and the transmission of property, both real and personal. * * * But if we are not yet emancipated, if we are still afloat on the fathomless abyss of metaphysical subtleties ; if we must steer our devious track among springing and secondary uses, resulting trusts, executory devises and cross remainders ; if the statute is subordinate only, and must be subjected to the ordeal, to the red hot ploughshares of the

Common Law, we are then in a situation infinitely worse than before the Revision. For if the statute is to be construed as in any way subordinate to the old system, there will then be a double conflict of technicalities, the Statute warring against the Common Law, and the Common Law against the Statute ; confusion will be worse confounded ; and every cause involving principles like the present will be an insoluble enigma.''

The determination of the Court of Errors to maintain in its integrity the new system originated by the Revised Statutes in reference to testamentary trusts and the alienation of estates was soon again exhibited in the decision upon the will of William James, of Albany, in the famous case of Hawley *vs.* James, reported in 5 Wendell, 317, and 16 Wendell, 61.

Here, as in the case of Lorillard's will, the decree of Chancellor Walworth, upholding the will in respect to its general scheme, was reversed and the main trusts declared void, as in violation of the Revised Statutes. Two of the Revisers, Mr. Butler and Mr. Spencer, were among the counsel in this case, and the opinions of the members of the Court are strong and clear in their declarations of an intent to give effect to the statutes controlling the case, wholly irrespective of antecedent rules or ideas.

Judge Bronson says :

'' To give effect to the statute in the spirit in which it was enacted, we must, as far as practicable, eradicate from our minds all that we have learned in relation to the doctrine of trusts as they existed before the late Revision. * * * We may resort to the Common Law for definition and rules of construction, where the statute itself is deficient. But in attempting to ascertain whether any particular trust can now be created, we cannot resort to the Common Law, for the obvious reason that this light has been extinguished by the Legislature.''

This wise and decisive action of the highest Court of the State gave the best assurance that the work of the Revision was a real reform which in al its essential features was to be permanent and perpetual.

It was accepted in the United States and in England as an expression and embodiment of the vital principles of the Common Law, practically adapted to the administration of a free government. It became the model of the Statutory system of other States and the pattern after which their laws were, in a large measure, modelled.

In the entertaining volume lately published by Walter Besant, entitled "Fifty Years Ago," the concluding chapter on "Law and Justice," prepared, as stated in the preface, by Mr. W. Morris Colles, of the Inner Temple, a graphic summary is given of the vast changes in the law of England during the Victorian half century. The era of legal reform he dates from the accession of the Queen, during whose reign of fifty years the whole fabric of judicial procedure has been reconstructed and many radical changes made in every department of the law. In 1837, when she came to the throne, there were nearly a thousand causes waiting to be heard in the Court of Chancery. In the second year of her reign nearly four thousand persons were arrested for debt in London alone, and of these nearly four hundred remained permanently in prison. The barbarism of the criminal law had been only partially mitigated. Practically nothing had been done to carry into effect the recommendations of the Parliamentary Law Reform Commission of 1826.

The Revised Statutes thus preceded by seven years the beginning of the reforms by which the administration of the law of Great Britain has been made to conform to the advance of civilization in other paths of progress.

The work was thus a guiding and controlling power in all the later movements of reform in the law.

In the State of New York it was the decisive step which kept her in the forefront of the jurisprudence of the nation, her place by right, to be maintained in the future, as in the past, by an honest and able Bar and a faithful and fearless Judiciary.

The many additions which have necessarily been engrafted upon the Revised Statutes in the course of the three score years of amazing progress and development, contained in the seven successive editions through which they have passed since their enactment have not changed the integrity of the original plan, or weakened in any essential part, the main structure.

The compensation paid by the State to the Revisers in addition to the sum of one thousand dollars voted to General Root on his retirement from the Commission was as follows : Mr. Wheaton received one thousand dollars, Mr. Duer and Mr. Spencer, each four thousand five hundred dollars. Mr. Butler, the only one of the persons originally appointed who continued to the end of the work received, owing to this circumstance, the larger sum of six thousand five hundred dollars ; a special compensation was allowed the two last named Revisers for preparing the table of contents, marginal notes and index, and superintending the publication of the whole work, in the sum of $1,000 each, and afterwards, for some special services, a further sum of $100 each was allowed.

If their task had been undertaken for its emoluments these would have been wholly inadequate, but the real reward came in the sense of the worthy performance of a momentous public trust and in the assured professional eminence accorded, and without any undue discrimination, to all of them.

From the work of these important years the Revisers advanced in maturer life to new honors in the profession and to high posts in the public service, State and National.

Their respective subsequent careers will be traced in the brief biographical sketches supplementing this narrative of the work of the revision, as a kind of *Postea* to the record now made up.

It is enough to say here that if the sole work of their lives had been that which we have now recalled, it would suffice to command our admiration and gratitude.

We may fitly apply to these associates in labors into

which the later toilers in the same fields, and we, in our own professional walks, have all entered, the weighty aphorism of Lord Bacon :

" If heaps on heaps of laws have swelled into so many volumes, or labor under such confusion, that it becomes necessary to reduce them into a healthy and active body, let this be a permanent concern ; let it be considered an heroic work ; and the authors of such a work should be solemnly and deservedly remembered among the legislators, among the founders of society."

In tracing the careers of the Revisers subsequent to the completion of their joint labors, I may be permitted to sketch briefly those of Chief Justice Duer and Mr. Spencer, and to reserve that of their associate for a final and fuller narrative.

The reasons for greater minuteness of detail in the concluding sketch will doubtless be as obvious to the reader as they are obligatory on my sense of duty. If further justification is needed, it may be found in the fact, already adverted to, that he was the sole member of the Commission who continued in it from its original creation in 1824 to the close of its labors in 1830, and who, from his residence during the entire period at the State capital, was most actively identified with the progress and consummation of the work.

In the case of his associates the materials for biography at my command are scanty, while the papers and correspondence of my father touch at many points not only personal but public affairs of great moment at the time to which they belong and of some historic value, and there is much in my personal recollections to aid in a portrayal of his character. Extended biographical details are, however, excluded by the plan of these commemorative sketches which are intended mainly to perpetuate whatever of interest attaches to their subjects in connection with their labors in the Revision and their services in later life to the State and Nation.

JOHN DUER, who, as we have seen, retired from the Commission before the completion of its labors, continued to discharge the duties of his office of United States District Attorney until the change of administration in 1828, when he resumed his private practice in the city of New York.

The versatility of his mind and his love of legal investigation led him to plan and execute, but only in part, an extended work on the law of Marine Insurance, a favorite subject of his study, with which his practice of commercial law had made him specially familiar.

The student of our earlier reports cannot fail to be struck with the number and importance of the cases argued and decided in the Supreme Court and the Court of Errors, during the time of those reports, involving questions of marine insurance. The leaders of the Bar of this city were masters of this branch of the law, which the growth of American commerce and the many complications arising out of the wars of Europe and our own later hostilities with Great Britain brought into operation in constantly occurring controversies. Mr. Duer's work was undertaken with the intention of covering, in three volumes, the entire subject of marine insurance; the first two volumes were published, successively, in 1845 and 1846. They were full of learning and ability, and were well received by the profession. For the full success of the work it was necessary that it should be completed, but the task of completion was never accomplished. An effort was made in 1848, by his warm friend and associate in the Revision, to ensure the preparation of the third volume by providing, in advance of its publication, a handsome return for the labor of completing the work and the generous manner in which this plan was entered upon by the leading members of the Metropolitan Bar showed the strong hold of Mr. Duer on the regard and affection of his fellow-laborers in the profession. In furtherance of this plan the sum of two thousand dollars was provided and paid to Benjamin F. Butler and Jonathan

Prescott Hall, but circumstances hindered the success of the effort and the trust fund reverted to the subscribers.

At the election for Judges of the Superior Court of the City of New York, held April 10, 1849, under the Act of March 24, 1849, to increase the number of Justices and to extend the jurisdiction of the Court, Mr. Duer was a successful candidate on the ticket of the Whig party, and after taking his seat on the Bench on May 2, 1849, all idea of completing his work on marine insurance seems to have been abandoned.

The election of Judge Duer gave general satisfaction to the profession, and placed him in a secure and agreeable position. The enlarged jurisdiction given to the Court, over which Samuel Jones and Thomas J. Oakley had in succession presided, and to which they and their associates had given the highest repute as a Court of commercial law, drew to it, under its enlarged jurisdiction, a great volume of business and cases of the first importance. To Judge Duer, the new duties he assumed were most congenial, and their discharge was marked by the personal charm of manner and the unvarying dignity which were always characteristic of him.

On May 16, 1857, he was elected Chief Justice of the Court, to fill the vacancy caused by the death of Chief Justice Oakley.

Between the great jurist, to whose place on the Bench he succeeded, and Judge Duer, there were many dissimilarities of mental traits and of intellectual tastes and pursuits, but a close friendship had existed between them, and in their judicial labors they united in upholding the highest standard of the administration of the law.

By natural constitution and temperament, Chief Justice Oakley was more a judge than an advocate, while Chief Justice Duer was rather an advocate than a judge, and they brought to bear on the hearing and determination of the causes submitted for their determination varied qualities and habits of mind, and very great learning and experience.

Chief Justice Oakley was terse and concise in his opinions, while his colleague was inclined to be more discursive and rhetorical.

Chief Justice Bosworth once told me that during the last days of Chief Justice Oakley's participation in the labors of the Court, in some instances he would express himself upon the cases assigned to him, orally, and his views would be reduced to writing by Judge Duer. In reading to him one of the opinions thus prepared, Judge Duer, after a discussion of the doubtful questions involved, came to the expression, "We are constrained to admit—" "Strike that out," said the "old Chief," as we were wont to call the veteran Chief Justice. "And what shall I put in its place?" asked his associate. "Say 'We think,'" was the quiet rejoinder, and the more judicial phrase passed into the opinion and the Reports.

During his term of office as Chief Justice, there were two occasions, one out of Court and one in Court, on which he showed conspicuously his warmth of feeling against what he deemed unwarrantable invasions of propriety.

In 1851, during the visit of Kossuth, the great Hungarian leader and orator, he attended a banquet given to this distinguished stranger by members of the Bar of New York. Kossuth, as the guest of the evening, in one of those impassioned speeches by which he roused the sympathies of the American people for the sufferings of the oppressed Hungarians, pushed to an extreme his appeal for interference by our government in their behalf, and easily evoked the after-dinner sympathy which is always available and abundant in an equal ratio to its irresponsibility. When the Judiciary came to be toasted, Judge Duer was called upon to respond, and while dealing with the Hungarian patriot in the most courteous and deferential manner, took occasion to denounce his efforts to seduce American citizens from the doctrine of non-interference with the affairs and controversies of foreign nations, inculcated by Washington, as a sowing of the seeds of political heresy and apostacy from the faith of the fathers of the Republic. The protest, we are told, "was received amid a storm of excitement." The incident caused much comment at the time, but was chiefly of importance as an exhibition of the courage and manliness with which Judge Duer could assert what he believed to be the right view of any great question without regard to the opposing feeling of the hour and at any risk of personal unpopularity or adverse criticism. This action of Judge Duer at the Kossuth dinner in New York was akin to a similar protest by Mr. Clay, when the Hungarian liberator sought an interview with him in his sick chamber at Washington, against any interference by the United States in aid of Hungary.*

The other instance was when a young man of the name of Finn, a lawyer by profession, conceived the idea that under the existing statutes in relation to the Superior Court a vacancy existed in the Bench which could be filled at a pending election.

Accordingly he prepared and printed a few ballots with his own name as candidate, distributed them among voters, and there being no opposing aspirant, claimed to have been elected as a Judge of the Court. He then made his appearance in the Court room, and asserted his right to be recognized as a member of the Court. As his claim was based upon the Statute, he supposed himself entitled to be regarded as having a *prima facie* right to civil treatment, at least, on the part of the Court of which he declared himself an Associate Justice. But Chief Justice Duer, looking upon the "claimant" as attempting to steal a judicial office from the people, as a trespasser *ab initio*, made short work of his clumsy pretensions. He would not tolerate Finn, or temporize with him or give him a standing in Court, or even a back seat on the Bench and the way in which the unfortunate aspirant for judicial honors vainly tried to maintain some show of a claim to act as a Judge of the Court under the unconcealed contempt and visible, honest indignation of the Chief Justice, was matter of con-

---

* Schurz' Life of Henry Clay, Vol. 2, p. 393.

siderable entertainment for the Bar and some activity on the part of the Court officers, and resulted in the utter discomfiture of the judicial pretender.

Chief Justice Duer died in the city of New York, August 8, 1858. The tributes paid to his memory by his brethren of the Bench and the Bar are contained in the sixth Volume of the Reports, published under his name, and exhibit in terms of warm and sincere eulogy the high estimation in which he was held by his associates and contemporaries.

Chief Justice Bosworth, his successor in office, a man singularly clear in judgment and cautious in expression, gave this testimony to his character and work as a Judge :

"No man was more industrious, or labored longer or more faithfully than he. He was so constituted that he could not be inactive. He read much, and probably, no Judge in the State read more promptly or with more care every elementary treatise and every volume of reports, from time to time as they were issued from the press. * *

No judicial opinions excel his own in clearness, in fullness of illustration, in beauty of style, in the vigor of their logic, or in the richness or variety of learning by which they are supported. However strong may have been the impressions he had formed in the argument of a cause, as the statement and argument of it presented it, if it so happened that these impressions had been formed in the absence from the mind of any fact which should justly affect the result, no one more readily than himself gave it its just effect when presented to his mind or recalled to his attention, and yielded so much of previous convictions as the truth and law of the case required. But when his conclusions were deliberately formed upon a consideration of all the facts and a careful examination of the law, they were, as all would expect, the conclusions of a man of strong mind and great learning should be, so fixed as not to be easily shaken.

He had another mental habit. I will not say it is peculiar, but it is not common, certainly not in the degree it characterized him. He rarely, if ever, attempted to write an opinion until his examination of a case, and of the authorities bearing upon it, had been fully made and completed. The mental process was pursued until no new thoughts were likely to occur from further reflection before he began to write. Writing was not to him an aid or assistant in the comparison of authorities, or in reaching the legal conclusions, which, together, they tended to establish. Hence, most of his opinions, even when delivered at length, were at the time unwritten. Hence, they were delivered with as much precision of language, and in a form nearly, if not quite, as perfect as he wrote. And when he came to write, it was rare that any page of the whole was disfigured with an alteration or an interlineation. I think it would surprise all who do not already know this fact, to inspect the manuscripts of his longest and most elaborate opinions. It is a rare occurrence that a word is obliterated, altered or interlined."

His colleague in the Revision, recalling their early association, added these words of personal attachment and glowing eulogy :

"In the labors and studies with Mr. Duer, to which I have referred, have been spent many of my happiest and most instructive days. For while we investigated, with a single eye to the good of our fellow-citizens and the glory of our profession, the whole body of our written law, and labored, through days and nights of toil, to give fit expression to those parts of it upon which we were employed, we lightened those toils by frequent excursions into other, and some times widely different walks. Considerably my senior in years, and far—very far—my superior in gifts and knowledge, he was in the law, and in every other department, emphatically 'my guide, philosopher and friend.' Not to speak of his lucid explanations of the ground and reason of the law, and the information he was so well qualified to give on legal questions continually coming into discussion in our daily tasks, he delighted to converse, not only on the more general topics of philosophy, politics and letters, but on the momentous questions which grow out of man's immortal nature, and the relations in which he stands to his Creator, Governor, and Judge. How great were his conversational powers! With what facility and richness he poured forth from the stores of his well-furnished mind, and by the aid of his powerful memory, wise and worthy thoughts and suggestions, on subjects which awakened those powers, must be well known to many of those now present ; indeed, to all who have had the opportunity of familiar intercourse with him. And now what shall I say more? When I think of the loss which you—brethren of the Bench and of the Bar—have all sustained—of the special loss which has fallen upon me—and of the far heavier loss which has fallen with crushing weight upon his afflicted family—I could almost cry out with one of old—

> " 'Quis desiderio sit pudor aut modus,
>   Tam cari capitis.' "

To these words of merited praise and as a fitting close to this brief memoir, must be added a few sentences from the speech on the same occasion by James T. Brady, the most eloquent and one of the ablest of the advocates of our Bar:

" He was a man of genius, and the spirit of the advocate which had been lighted up by that genius in his early professional career never quitted him, even on the Bench, and it would be flattery to say that this was not one of his characteristics. But he was the high advocate of right, of law, of justice. It is true, that when a case was brought before the Bench to be discussed, and that there was advanced even one thought that seemed to be the precursor of error coming to cloud or confuse the judicial mind, he never hesitated to expose or expel it. It is true that he stood as with a flaming sword, and guarded every entrance by which such error might approach. It is true that his mind caught from the discussion, which elicited sparks of flashing intelligence from the members of the Bar, many a ray of parti-colored light. In that respect the gem set within his soul suggested a close comparison to another jewel highly prized among men. It could give back all the tints cast upon it; but it remained still the diamond—brilliant in its pure integrity with its singleness of color and its capacity to diffuse more light than its face received."

Chief Justice Duer married in 1804, Anne Bedford Bunner, daughter of George Bunner; she survived her husband and died December 26, 1864.

JOHN C. SPENCER, on the completion of his share in the work of the Revision, was appointed in 1829, by Martin Van Buren, then Governor, the prosecuting officer, on behalf of the State, of the supposed abductors of William Morgan, a bricklayer living at Batavia, Genesee county, N. Y., who had been taken by a body of men in September, 1826, from the jail at Canandaigua and carried thence to the Niagara river, in whose waters he was believed to have been drowned by his captors, all in revenge for his alleged disclosures of secrets of the Masonic order.

Morgan's case and the prosecution of the persons charged with complicity in his taking off were controlling elements in the political struggles of the time in which they happened. The rise, progress and extinction of the Anti-Masonic party belong to the curiosities of political history. It seems strange to us, in the retrospect, that hostility to a private society should have become the basis of a State party and ultimately of a National party attaining such proportions as to induce this deliberate statement by John Quincy Adams in one of the innumerable entries in his diary: "The dissolution of the Masonic institution in the United States I believe to be more important to us and our posterity than the question whether Mr. Clay or General Jackson shall be President."

William Wirt, the brilliant and versatile Attorney-General, first appointed by Mr. Monroe in 1819 and continued in office by Mr. Adams, was nominated for the Presidency in 1828 as an Anti-Masonic candidate, and as the result of what he himself called "a political scrape," and what seems in the retrospect almost a senseless escapade, carried a single State, Vermont, General Jackson being elected President by 219 electoral votes over Mr. Clay, who received only 49 votes.

Mr. Spencer's efforts as prosecuting officer against the Masonic ringleaders were honest and fearless but with no very marked results. Their conspiracy had been only too well contrived and executed. He espoused the Anti-Masonic cause as a politician as well as an attorney, perhaps to show that he was as sincere in his desire to destroy the influence of the Masonic order as he was to convict the perpetrators of the crime which had made it obnoxious. He supported Wirt for the Presidency, was on the Anti-Masonic electoral ticket in New York and suffered defeat with his party.

The Whig party rose on the ruins of the Anti-Masonic movement and rapidly consolidated the varying elements of opposition to the administration of General Jackson, whose strong and aggressive policy coerced the minority into cohesion and organized opposition under their ablest leaders. Mr. Spencer gave in his adhesion, but remained in private life until 1838, when William H. Seward was elected Governor, and Mr. Spencer, having in 1837 removed his residence to Albany, was elected, on the same ticket, as Secretary of State. Being *ex-officio* Superintendent of Common Schools, he took up anew the subject of education as connected with the State and by a masterly report exhibited his thorough acquaintance with the whole subject of public instruction.

In the succession of Mr. Tyler to the presidency after General Harrison's death, in April, 1841, Mr. Spencer became a member of his Cabinet as Secretary of War, and later was appointed Secretary of the Treasury. His adhesion to President Tyler's political fortunes cost him his position as a leader of the Whig party, and when his name was sent to the Senate by the President, as the nominee for the vacant place on the bench of the Supreme Court, caused by the death of Justice Smith Thompson, his rejection was the logical consequence of the hostility engendered by his close relations with the President.

Mr. Spencer's political career closed with his retirement from the Treasury and his declared opposition to the annexation of Texas. The remaining years of his life were spent in the practice of the law at Albany, where he died May 20, 1854. He had married, May 20, 1809, Elizabeth Scott Smith, who survived him and who died October 10, 1869.

Mr. Spencer's death closed a serviceable and patriotic career, meriting even higher recognition than has been accorded it. But he was less fortunate in forming political alliances than in the exercise of his native gifts. Probably no member of the Bar of this State ever brought to the work of the profession greater faculties of insight and endurance. His mind has been fitly characterized as "gigantic in its comprehension and microscopic in its accuracy." Of this class of intellects a conspicuous example in our own later time was furnished by Charles O'Conor, a man who in many of his intellectual traits and in some of his idiosyncrasies of political opinion resembled Mr. Spencer, of whom he was a great admirer. He specially praised his method of argument and his rare power of coming at once and with absolute precision to "the real point of the case."

Mr. Spencer was a man of the deepest convictions, stern, sometimes repulsive in his assertion of them, tenacious and fearless alike in the friendships, and in the antagonisms of life, strong, resolute and iron-willed, and yet kindly and sympathetic in his nature.

The general judgment of the profession was summed up in the brief sentence of a journalist who characterized his "singular capacity to labor without fatigue as only equalled by the extent and variety of the professional services he performed."

———

BENJAMIN F. BUTLER, who survived both his associates in the work of the Revision, and who alone had been identified with it from its earliest inception to its close, was justly accorded a large share of the professional repute which accrued to its authors.

His residence at Albany and his connection with the leaders of the political party then firmly established in power both in the State of New York and in the Federal government, as well as his assured professional rank, combined to place him at the front of the Bar.

In the Court of Errors he was constantly employed in the most important causes. At the session held in New York in 1833, of the whole number of eighteen cases reported in the 11th volume of Wendell's Reports, he was counsel in nine, including the well known case of Grover *vs.* Wakeman establishing the right of an insolvent debtor to make preferences, in good faith, in an assignment for creditors, and the leading case of Allen *vs.* Addington establishing the liability of a third party making representations by means of which a purchaser obtains credit from a vendor.

I find a home-letter written during his attendance at this term of the Court of Errors, in which he says that he is glad to have an associate counsel in one of his many cases, as he fears the Court will weary of hearing continuous arguments by himself.

His relations at this time to the Bench and the Bar of the State were particularly agreeable. The means of access to the capital from remote and interior points and, during the winter season, even from New York, were so inadequate in comparison with those now existing, that a journey to Albany was a serious affair, and at the sessions of the courts held there the employment of local counsel was far more frequent than now. Of the practice thus created he enjoyed a very large share. He occupied, while he remained at Albany, a position in this regard similar to that afterwards enjoyed by Nicholas Hill, one of the brightest ornaments of the Bar of this State and its most conspicuous leader in the court of last resort.

In February, 1833, on the retirement from the United States Senate of William L. Marcy to assume the office of Governor of the State of New York, the vacant place in the Senate was urgently pressed on Mr. Butler, and Mr. Van Buren, then Vice-President and the presumptive candidate for the Presidency in 1836, desired him to accept it.

But he was firm is his resolution to take no office which would withdraw him from his professional pursuits.

Governor Marcy afterwards desired to appoint him to the Bench of the Supreme Court, as the successor of Judge Sutherland. Chief Justice Savage, who presided in the Court during the whole period of the Revision, and for six years after its completion, wrote him a letter communicating the offer, and urging its acceptance in these words of warm personal friendship—

"The office of Judge, permit me to say, is one to which you are well adapted ; and in which you can render as great service to your native State as any other. It is one in which you will probably enjoy as much human happiness as any other, and in which you will have as much leisure for literary pursuits, perhaps, as in the duties of an arduous profession ; and supposing you to have, as all members of the profession ought to have, a laudable ambition for an elevated standing as a jurist and scholar, in which of the walks of learning can you have a better field for the exercise of your powers? This is a subject on which I need not attempt to persuade you ; you must act as your judgment directs. I will only remark farther, that should you accept the office, there is every probability that in a few years at farthest you will preside in the Court. And I need not inform you that, in my estimation, that station is as honorable as any in our State, and is surpassed by but few in the United States."

But the Chief Justice, with the candor and fairness which characterized him, did not fail to point out to his friend that unless he already had money in his purse sufficient for his future wants, the judicial office was to be shunned. The want of a proper compensation for his services had driven Judge Sutherland from the Bench which he adorned, and the Chief Justice, referring to this circumstance, says, "the cause of that resignation is rather calculated to deter those who are most competent to fill the vacancy from accepting the station. Indeed, if a man wishes to be rich he should become so before he ascends the Bench."

The meagre pittance then allowed by the State to our Supreme Court Judges was of itself a bar to the judicial office to a man with a large family and an ample professional practice, and the place on the Bench was declined. Fortunately for the State, an incumbent was found so situated as to be able to accept the vacant seat, and so endowed with rare judicial qualities as to make his long and conspicuous career in the Supreme Court of the State, and afterwards is the Supreme Court of the United States, one of the most noted examples of eminence and fidelity in the annals of the American judiciary.

In February, 1833, Peter A. Jay and Benjamin F. Butler, of New York, were appointed, with Theodore Frelinghuysen, of New Jersey, a commission to settle the long-disputed controversy of half a century's duration as to the boundary line between the two States, a service resulting in the convention which has ever since controlled the jurisdiction and rights of these States as respects their boundary line.

Meanwhile, repeated overtures came to Mr. Butler from Washington, through Mr. Van Buren, looking to his acceptance of office in the Administration of General Jackson. These were declined as often as they were renewed until, in the great political crisis caused by the struggle between the national administration and the Bank of the United States, the summons to Washington seemed so imperative that it could not be refused without apparently placing personal considerations above public duty.

Up to this time the whole tenor of his life had been undisturbed by any influences foreign to his position as a leader of the Bar of his native State and to an active interest in the stirring public questions of the time. His friendship for Mr. Van Buren had kept him in close alliance with the political party of which his former partner was the acknowledged head, and in co-operation with Governor Marcy, Edwin Croswell, Azariah C. Flagg, Silas Wright,

John A. Dix and the other leading public men of the Capitol, who, from their union in political action, had acquired the sobriquet of the "Albany Regency."

This union, though generally supposed to be for the advancement of party objects, was, in fact, largely due to a community of views on what the men who formed it regarded the true principles of free democratic government. Their unselfish and undeviating personal regard for Mr. Van Buren was something remarkable and rare in political fellowships. His high gift and faculty of attaching to himself, by strong ties of friendship, able and upright men, has been well cited by his latest biographer as a proof of the intrinsic worth of his character.

To those persons who imagine that the chief aim of men who by nature and association incline to active participation in public affairs, is the possession of place and power, the letters which passed between Mr. Van Buren and his former pupil and devoted friend touching the acceptance by the latter of high office in the National Government, would go far toward correcting such an impression. It needed every argument and appeal which the older man was able to present to the younger to overcome his reluctance to leave his private professional life for a more public career.

Devoted to the pursuits of a student, he delighted in nothing so much as in scholarly habits and in imparting to others the knowledge he had acquired, reminding me in these traits of the ardent love of research so conspicuous in Sir William Jones, whom he greatly resembled in character and whose expressed desire was to retire, at the close of his professional life, to the retreat of his beloved University, there to pursue without interruption the studies which were his chief enjoyment.

He had already given thought to the plan of a Law School and always preferred the task of studying and teaching the law, as a science, to any other pursuit. With these views he had steadily put aside all offers of public office, greatly strengthened in this course of action by the strong repugnance of his wife to the society and life of the Federal Capital.

He had married in 1818, just after his admssion to the Bar, Harriet Allen, the daughter of Howard and Lydia Allen, who were among the Nantucket Colony which founded the city of Hudson, N. Y., and whose son, William Howard Allen, after a brilliant career in the United States Navy, distinguishing himself in the engagement between the Argus and the Pelican in the war of 1812, had been killed in the service while attacking a piratical vessel in the West India seas.

His name has been immortalized by the Muse of Halleck.

I cannot forbear citing here one of Mr. Van Buren's letters as an illustration of his friendship and consideration, and of the tone and temper in which he treated the personal, local and moral aspects of the subject he discussed. Written at a moment when he was himself the subject of coarse ridicule and vituperation, based on incessant charges of the selfish and sinister motives which the political opponents who envied his success and plotted for his defeat never wearied of imputing to him, it shows the exercise of qualities as far removed from the duplicity of political intrigue as his pure personal character and fidelity to duty were alien to the low instincts of his traducers.

WASHINGTON, November, 8, 1833.

MY DEAR SIR :

I bespeak for the proposition I am about to make yours and Mrs. Butler's most deliberate consideration, before you conclude to reject it. I say Mrs. B's, because in whatever relates so essentially to your future welfare, she ought of right to be consulted ; and she has on a former occasion shown herself so much wiser than we were, that it would be a positive injustice to refuse to take her into counsel now.

The appointment of Mr. Daniel to the office of Attorney-General was published by mistake, before his positive acceptance had been ascertained. He has been with us, and after a full and frank conversation with the President, has decided not to accept it. With the reasons for that decision, which he came to with the greatest pain and reluctance, it is unnecessary, now, to trouble you. Mr. Daniel is a gentleman of the very highest character, and very respectable talents, but does not entertain that confidence in them which his friends think would be justifiable ; and there were urgent family and personal obstacles. The President thought, as I informed you, that he ought to go South for this appointment, and having in good faith done so, he will now regard the accidental circumstance of the publication of Mr. Daniel's appointment a fortunate incident, if it shall, as he hopes, enable him to bring into his cabinet one who every member of it would be delighted to see here, and that is yourself. Before this had occurred, I would not myself have proposed it to you, had the matter been at my disposal. Now, I think it free from difficulty or objection. The President will with the greatest pleasure confer the appointment upon you, and I am as solicitous as I could possibly be upon any subject that you shall accept it. Independent of the public considerations which are amply sufficient to justify this solicitude, I feel that if not indispensable, (though extremely important,) for the present, it is, in reference to a possible future, most fitting as it respects myself that you should be here in some such a situation. Not one word is necessary, I know, to satisfy you that I would not press my personal solicitude upon you, as I for the first time freely do, if I were not entirely satisfied, that what I ask of you will promote your own interests, and those of your family ; or at the least that it will certainly not prejudice them. I think so in respect to all the points, which, in such a case arise for consideration, and I will briefly assign my reasons. Although you will recollect, I readily concurred in your objection to taking the place of Senator, I have ever since been impressed with the belief that it was a sacrifice which you might with propriety have made. I gave in to your views, partly because I feared that from your gentlemanly and pacific disposition (although not wanting in spirit when its exhibition is necessary), the rough and tumble of the Senate might not please you ; but principally, because I was apprehensive that it might affect the interests of your family in a pecuniary point of view. That now presented steers entirely clear of these objections, and has advantages which ought not to be lightly overlooked. Although you are not the slave of mad ambition, you are, as you ought to be, tenacious of your professional standing. That cannot be increased at home, and can only be made *National*, by becoming identified with National concerns. Depend upon it, my dear sir, that this is so. The fact presses itself upon my observation almost daily, when I find how little is known, or cared, abroad, about you who are at the very top of the ladder at home. Mr. Wirt, Mr. Webster, Mr. Pinkney and Mr. Taney, although possessing the same talents, would not have gone beyond a passing observation out of their own States, if they had not entered upon the National theatre. You recollect to have merely heard of Mr. Taney, whilst at the Washington Bar, now, although the same man, he is known and respected as a man of talents throughout the Union. The reason why it is so, it is unnecessary to go into ; the fact is sufficient and undeniable, that the great body of the people, will only look for the great men of the *Nation* amongst those who are actually engaged in its service. Although you are too wise to be craving for a distinction of this sort, you are at the same time too wise to be indifferent to it. Providence has cut you out for its acquisition in this very place, and you have no right to turn your back upon the occasion, which presents it to you in so honorable and entirely unexceptionable a manner. In a pecuniary point of view, it cannot, I deliberately think, be otherwise than beneficial. The salary is $4,500, besides office, messenger, clerks, &c., and occasional compensation from the Government for services which do not necessarily appertain to the office. You can enter upon the business of the Supreme Court of the U. S. with advantages, which, if not immediately equal to those of Webster (who makes his thousands not to say tens of thousands by it), very soon would be ; and the President says it will be competent for you, without prejudice to the public interest, to attend the higher Courts at New York and Albany. All previous Atty. Genls., who desired it, have done so in respect to their own States. To the former place you will, next season, be able to go in 15 hours, and to the latter in a day and a night. What, then, is there to prevent you from increasing your provision for your children, which I admit to be obligatory on you ? Nothing that I can see. You can live as cheap here as in N. York. Your manner of living can be regulated by your own taste, and as everybody knows that you are not a man of pleasure, or parade, nobody will gossip about you. By taking this course, you will accomplish what you are all so anxious about—viz., that you can be more with your family than heretofore.

The only exception need be, your visits to N. York during the sittings of the Courts, when you can take your family with you, without stopping between this and N. Y., especially when the railroad, the making of which is now under full operation, is completed. I recollect when the subject was before contingently discussed, and when you concluded that you could not take it, that Mrs. Butler did not like the idea of bringing her daughters up here. Upon reflection, I think she will find that objection not so well founded as she then supposed. Mr. McLean, Mr. Taney, Mr. Woodbury and Gov. Cass have each a houseful of little girls of the very finest character, and I am quite sure that the society for Mrs. B. and the children would be at least as good here as in N. York ; *and if she cannot possibly do without hearing something more upon the subject of temperance*, she can count upon Gov. Cass as a never-failing source. He has as much of the true spirit in him as Norton and Delavan combined, and Mr. Van Vechten and Courtland Van Rensselaer to boot. But to return from this digression, you must come. I tell you frankly that I have made up my mind so decidedly that it is best for the public, for you and yours, for myself, and that you will prove to be useful and acceptable to the President, that I cannot think of a declension with composure. As you were willing, in the exuberance of friendship, to come with me in 1829 as Under Secretary, and give up the finest professional prospects man ever had, I shall think you must have undergone some strange metamorphosis, if you now refuse to come into the Cabinet with those professional prospects enhanced instead of abandoned. This must in the first instance be strictly confined to Mr. and Mrs. Flagg, Croswell, Dix and John, with whom I wish you to advise. If, contrary to my earnest hope, you determine to decline, not a word must be said upon the subject. If you act the wiser part, you may, as is usual in such cases, consult with your friends generally after your mind is made up. I have not included the Governor, because he is, I suppose, busy with his message, but you may speak to him, of course, if you wish it. Tell Mrs. B. I shall never forgive her if she throws any obstacles in the way. I intend to be in N. York on Wednesday of next week, and hope you will meet me there.

It will, in case of acceptance, be necessary that you should come down immediately, for a day or two only, to sign some patents which are waiting the Atty. Gen'l's signature, and there is no authority to appoint an acting Atty. After that, you may return and make your arrangements for the winter. If you conclude, as you ought to do, I wish you would write at once to the President, as he is very anxious to have the matter closed.

Remember me very kindly to Mrs. B. and the children, and believe me,

Very truly yours,

M. Van Buren.

To

B. F. Butler, Esq.

P. S.—The President has read this letter, and approves it. He does not write you himself because I have told him that it is not necessary at this time.

M. V. B."

The appeal thus made could not be withstood and a letter was written to President Jackson, accepting the office of Attorney-General, on the duties of which the new incumbent immediately entered.

The hold which he had upon the community in which his lot had been cast, is shown by the letter written to him on his leaving Albany, signed by leading citizens of all pursuits and parties. It is dated November 26, 1833, and bears eighty-nine signatures, the names including many of the most eminent citizens of the State, familiar in its history as statesmen, judges, lawyers, divines, physicians and men of note in various walks, and testifies to their estimate of his worth, their personal friendship and their regret at losing him from their social circles and from active co-operation in the interests of the city.

In Albany he had been foremost in every good work, and especially enthusiastic in the cause of Temperance, at a time when organized efforts in its behalf were in their earliest stage. Edward C. Delavan, whose long and active career as a Temperance leader, has given him a high place as a philanthropist, was a co-worker with him in a crusade against the use of ardent spirits, an evil unfortunately conspicuous at Albany, especially during the Legislative sessions, and a prolific source of painful public and private scandals.

The presence of strong drink in the form of New England rum and Holland gin, on sideboards and dining tables, and the almost universal habit of tippling in private houses as well as taverns, sanctioned by the Common Law of hospitality derived from both the English and Dutch ancestors of the good people of Albany, was thoroughly established. Against this dangerous and destructive habit, a few reformers took their stand and set on foot an energetic movement, which developed into the concerted action of State and National societies.

Mr. Delavan, who was able to give an almost exclusive devotion to the reform he had so much at heart, went to an extreme in its advocacy by asserting abstinence, and not temperance, as the rule of social duty and even as a necessary canon of Christian practice. With characteristic ardor he emptied the contents of his wine cellar into the gutter of Washington street, in front of his homestead, as a libation on the altar of his new found faith, an offering as sincere as it was eccentric.

At this point the co-reformers parted company. At Albany and afterwards at Washington, while Mr. Delavan was pushing the cause of total abstinence, his former associate advocated that of temperance, holding to the end of his life the views he had matured in his earlier study of the subject, to which he had given the same thorough and conscientious research which he brought to every topic engaging his attention.

Mr. Delavan, in his desire to bring his friend into unison with his extreme views, placed in his hands a work by an English clergyman, in which the scriptural argument for abstinence was mainly grounded on the difference between the Hebrew words employed in the Old Testament to denote " wine " or " strong drink," where the use was commended, and the words employed where the use was condemned, the former words referring to unfermented or non-intoxicating juice of the grape, and the latter to intoxicating drinks. The author came to this country and made a visit to Mr. Delavan, who, in advance of his arrival, notified Mr. Butler of his coming, and arranged that an interview should take place between them. To this interview he looked forward with certain anticipation of the conversion of his friend to his own views.

During the interval, the latter subjected the book and its argument to the most thorough examination. Bible in hand, he scrutinized every passage in the Old Testament in which, in the authorized version, the words "wine" or "strong drink" occur, and prepared a complete "brief," as to the use of the word in the English translation, a task which I well remember occupied the leisure of the Sundays of a summer vacation.

The author arrived, and the interview which Mr. Delavan had arranged took place at his office in Albany. The sequel may be best told in his own words, taken from a letter which he wrote me after my father's death, in reference to this episode in the course of their long and unbroken friendship. He says:

"The meeting of these two learned Christian men was to me of the deepest interest, for I saw that if Dr. James could be sustained, the cause would be placed on the most impregnable basis, on God's Word, and nothing could overthrow it. For some time it appeared that all things were going on smoothly to sustain Dr. James, but all at once your father came to a text where *Yayin* was introduced. 'Now tell me, Dr. James,' said your father, ' does *Yayin* here mean intoxicating wine?' I saw, at once, my friend Dr. James appeared to be confused, if not confounded, the blood mounted to his face, and he declined to answer to your father's satisfaction, who at once rolled up his papers and left the office, and I have no doubt he then made up his mind that we must look elsewhere than to the Bible as authority for total abstinence as a duty."

Mr. Delavan, while conceding that the argument of his author did not stand the test of thorough investigation, was always unwilling to admit that the untoward result described in his letter was due to anything else than an unwillingness on the part of Dr. James to acknowledge an error which was capable of explanation, and which, as Mr. Delavan further on in the letter from which I have quoted, and in conversation, insisted, was by no means fatal to the Scriptural argument. But the Bible study in preparation for the discussion, perhaps more than the discussion itself, the result of which so disappointed Mr. Delavan, led to settled convictions on the part of his friend, and confirmed him in the habit of temperance, pursued with a strictness which, while rejecting compulsory extremes, was so consistent and absolute as to entitle him to the tribute of another life-long friend, that he exemplified the lines of Dryden, and

> " Refined himself to soul, to curb the sense,
> And almost made a sin of abstinence."

In a letter in my possession, written by General Jackson to Mr. Van Buren, he says that the new Attorney-General has made a visit to Washington and produced a very favorable impression.

The first impression thus recorded deepened into the warmest friendship. The intimacy between the President and the Attorney-General became close and familiar, and seemed to be nourished and strengthened by the absolute dissimilarity of their training and characteristics. The old soldier of the frontier and the wilderness—choleric and self-willed, violent in opinion and prejudice, but sound in sense and in the principles he held, patriotic to the core, and fearless of any foe—had a sympathetic side to his rough-hewn nature which only revealed itself at the magic touch of a true and loyal friendship. Such a friendship was soon formed between the youngest member of the Cabinet and the veteran President. The most unreserved confidence and personal attachment existed between them. The political gossip which affixed to the duties of the Attorney-General that of the President's " conscience-keeper "—while meant for a partisan sneer—was not wholly a misnomer, for the function of conscience was neither out of place nor out of use in the sharp conflicts of that political era.

Whatever may be the final judgment as to the right or wrong of the opposing views and the contending parties of the time, the men who rallied to the support of Jackson against Nullification, against the domination of the United States Bank and the diversion of the Government from the simple province of governing, will suffer nothing by comparison with their opponents, either as to purity of private character or patriotism in the discharge of public duty.

Necessarily, to a man accustomed by long habit and native choice to do more work than duty required, the labors of the office of Attorney-General did not wholly suffice. It had not, at that time, reached the proportions of the present Department of Justice, and the salary was wholly inadequate to the expenses of a life in Washington. But, while preparing and arguing, without aid, all the Government causes and discharging all the other duties of the office, these were supplemented by a continued private practice in the higher Courts, State and Federal.

At the close of the Seminole War, in 1836, when General Cass left the War Department for the mission to France, President Jackson, anticipating the election of Mr. Van Buren to the Presidency, and wishing to leave him free to select the successor of General Cass, insisted, in a personal letter, that, for the remainder of the term, the Attorney-General should assume the duties of the vacant office.

He wrote as follows :

"WASHINGTON, Oct. 4, 1836.

MY DEAR SIR : Governor Cass has this day handed me his resignation and I have appointed Mr. Harris to act as Secretary of War until another is appointed.

From the conversation I had with you on this subject I rely upon your taking charge of that Department until the 4th of March next. This combined with your duty as Attorney-General will be onerous, still I know your capacity and indefatigable industry, competent to both, and as far as my abilities and health will permit, the burden shall be lightened.

Please present me kindly to your amiable lady and family and accept the assurance of my continued respect, confidence and esteem.

ANDREW JACKSON."

The office of Secretary of War was accordingly accepted and its duties discharged until the close of President Jackson's term.

It was during this short incumbency that the sole instance of conflict between the Cabinet officer and the Executive occurred. A West Point cadet had been dismissed from the Academy, on sufficient grounds, by the Superintendent of the post and the case was before the Secretary of War for his action. Some personal friends of the offender went to President Jackson and made so strong an appeal to him, that he yielded good naturedly to their intercession and made an order reinstating the dismissed cadet. The Secretary of War at once insisted that this order was an interference with his proper duties, calling for his resignation, if not promptly withdrawn. The President saw his mistake and revoked his order.

On the accession of Mr. VanBuren to the Presidency, he was more than ready to place his old pupil and steadfast friend at the head of any Department of the Government he might prefer and would not listen to his request for retirement. The favorite project of a Law School retained its hold on his sympathies and he had already made an engagement to undertake the establishment of a Law Department in the University of the City of New York, whose liberal charter granted by the Legislature of 1833 gave it power to embrace a course of legal studies in its various branches of instruction. Adhering to his determination to accept no position which was non-professional, he yielded to Mr. Van Buren's wishes by agreeing to retain the office of Attorney General for a year, a period afterwards lengthened by six months, and on September 15, 1838, his resignation was reluctantly accepted by the President, whose letter accepting it is marked by the same kindness and consideration as that already given to the reader. He says : "However deep my regret at parting with you, I am nevertheless too well satisfied that justice to yourself and your family, require this step on your part, to hesitate in complying with your wishes."

The commercial disasters of 1836 and 1837 and the consequent period of financial disorder and distress had caused wide-spread embarrassments from which professional men were not wholly exempt and public office with its attendant burden of expense was undesirable and in fact impossible in comparison with the advantages of a leading professional position in New York. Before his retirement from the Cabinet of Mr. Van Buren, the Attorney-General had settled his family in New York and on his return to private life he entered at once into active practice at the Metropolitan Bar.

At the same time he undertook the execution of his long cherished plan of a Law School.

William Kent, then high in professional eminence and David Graham, Jr., one of the most brilliant members of the New York Bar, a man of the highest repute for his success before juries both in the civil and criminal courts, and author of a standard work on Practice, associated themselves with him in the work.

Doctor James M. Matthews, a prominent divine and a man of great executive capacity and unbounded confidence in the success of the extended plans he had formed for the University of which he was a main promoter and the first Chancellor, had succeeded in enlisting the co-operation of many leading men in the organization of an institution, which was intended to found in the great commercial and business centre of the nation, a true University, embracing courses of instruction in every department of art and science, with the great advantages to be derived from the constantly growing resources of the metropolis and a broad and free system of management and control, suited to the commercial genius as well as the political methods of the people.

The experiment of a Law School undertaken with many auspices of success was environed by some insuperable obstacles.

Like many of the enterprises of that period, full of grand schemes hindered by the financial misfortunes which had overspread the country, a long period of patient waiting and working was required to bring to a successful issue the plans of its founders.

The Law Department was inauguarated by addresses delivered by the three professors early in 1838, and a complete course of instruction was marked out, most admirable in its conception and details, and some students were at once attracted to the courses of instruction. But this experiment of conducting a School of Law by lectures to be delivered by lawyers in full practice at the Bar, and to be listened to by students in law offices, was, at the time it was tried, premature and impossible of success.

The co-workers in this earliest effort to establish a School of Law, could only lay the foundations on which in after years their successors have been able, with ampler sources of success, to build with honor and profit.

Shortly after Mr. Butler's return to New York, the sudden death by his own hand, of William M. Price, the District Attorney for the Southern District of New York, startled the profession and alarmed the Government. President Van Buren, who wished to place the office in strong and safe hands, immediately asked the ex-Attorney General to accept it. It was an office at that time peculiarly representative of the Government. John Duer, his Associate Reviser, had held it under Mr. Adams. It did not preclude private practice in the Courts, and was liberally compensated by the fees allowed by law in lieu of salary, and was regarded by the profession as a post of high distinction. This office he held during the whole of Mr. Van Buren's term, being succeeded by

Ogden Hoffman on the accession of General Harrison, March 4th, 1841.

Mr. Van Buren's defeat at the Presidential election of 1840, did not in the least dampen the ardor of his political friends in New York, and they looked forward with certainty to his continued leadership of the Democratic party, and to his candidacy in 1844.

In the Convention, held at Baltimore, in May, 1844, Mr. Butler as the nearest personal friend of Mr. Van Buren and his immediate political representative, headed the opposition to the scheme by which, under the imposition of the rule requiring a two-thirds vote to nominate the candidate, the clear majority pledged to Mr. Van Buren, in advance of the Convention, was rendered wholly ineffectual.

His speech at Baltimore in opposition to the two-thirds rule, I think he regarded as the most important oratorical effort of his life. Always a graceful and persuasive speaker, he was, when aroused by a special subject or occasion, impassioned and eloquent. In this instance, the discovery of what he deemed a plot contrived to defraud its victim of an ascertained majority vote by making the vote itself instrumental to destroy its efficacy as a controlling force, coupled with his strong personal attachment to the chief whose downfall this treachery was meant to compass, gave to his effort the daring of a brave soldier caught, with his leader, in a traitorous ambuscade, and fighting for a life dearer than his own. All descriptions of the scene concur in giving this impression of his bold, vigorous but unavailing defense of the right of the majority.

The claims of Mr. Van Buren to the continued leadership of his party were inconsistent with the plans of the managers of the Southern Democracy. These had been thoroughly matured, and they admitted of no candidacy which was not in full sympathy with the demand for the annexation of Texas, to which Mr. Van Buren had refused his concurrence, at the risk of losing the nomination for the Presidency. The Southern leaders succeeded in that part of their scheme which called for the defeat of Van Buren, but failed in that part of it which called for the nomination of the candidate they opposed to him. A letter from Mr. Van Buren to Mr. Butler withdrawing his name was followed by the capture of the Convention for a nominee to whom the Van Buren men transferred their votes, James K. Polk, who had been favored by them as a candidate for the Vice-Presidency, and whose friends, finding him available to unite the requisite two-thirds of the convention, eagerly fell in with his nomination for the higher office, which was followed by his election, in November, 1844.

Mr. Polk pressed upon Mr. Butler a seat in his Cabinet, and the leading friends of Mr. Van Buren urged him to accept it, but he had no disposition to return to Washington, especially as the associations of his former residence could not be renewed, and he contented himself with resuming, at the President's solicitation, the District Attorneyship in New York, a position which he occupied until the Spring of 1848, when the growing aggressions of the Slave Power and the subserviency of the national administration to its demands aroused his indignation, severed his long relations with the Democratic party and brought him into open hostility to the Administration and its measures.

The Free-Soil Convention, held at Buffalo in August, 1848, marked the uprising of the spirit of genuine resistance on the part of the North to the domination of the Slave Power. It was a movement wholly within the lines of the Constitution, uninfluenced and uncontrolled by men of extreme views, and having for its real, as well as its declared purpose, the reassertion in principle and in the practical administration of the government of the nationality of freedom and the sectionalism of slavery, by its absolute exclusion from the Territories and from the new States. "No more slave States, and no slave Territory," was a plain declaration, and while it violated no constitutional guaranty or right, it was the death knell of the supremacy of the Southern oligarchy which sought to rule the nation. Into this movement Mr. Butler entered with all the enthusiasm of his earlier days, and with entire unselfishness and patriotism.

He was largely instrumental in bringing about the candidacy of Van Buren and Adams for President and Vice-President upon the Free-Soil platform of 1848, a candidacy consistent with the faith of the fathers and founders of the Democratic party, and the only possible protest on the part of those who, while holding its principles of government, had never entered into alliance with the propagandism of slavery.

The defeat of the Democratic ticket, the election of General Taylor, and the exclusion of slavery from California and New Mexico followed, with the seeming pacification of the slavery agitation by the compromises of 1850, effected by the powerful aid of Mr. Webster, for himself, however patriotic in intent, a fatal lapse, and for the country a delusive truce.

In July, 1849, Governor Fish sent Mr. Butler an appointment as "Commissioner of the Code," requesting his co-operation in the work of codification then in progress, but this was declined and his whole time was given to his private practice and to the philanthropic objects in which he was interested.

The nomination for the Presidency, in 1852, of Franklin Pierce, a native of New Hampshire, gave to the Free-Soil Democrats of 1848 some ground of hope for an administration on a patriotic basis. The compromise measures had taken effect as a kind of stay of proceedings to prevent extreme action by either party and there was no emergency to arouse the spirit of the North to renewed activity against the Slave Power. The Democratic Free-Soil leaders deemed it safer to adhere to the old party than to venture on the extreme and doubtful ground occupied by the promoters of the candidacy of Hale and Julian. Salmon P. Chase, in an open letter to Mr. Butler appealed to him to oppose the Democratic ticket, but he replied, August 7, 1852, by a letter in which he reviewed the whole political situation, declared his adhesion to the principles of the Free-Soil Convention, and avowed his intention of supporting Pierce and King, as representing sound Democratic doctrines and whose election under the existing state of things he believed would place the whole responsibility of the government in the hands of the Democratic party, who, if they should lend themselves to a crusade against Freedom would soon be justly overthrown.

Personal attachment to General Pierce had something to do with this adhesion to him as a candidate. He had been a Representative in Congress from New Hampshire during General Jackson's administration, and a warm friendship, based on identity of literary tastes, had sprung up between him and the Attorney-General. I well remember the evening on which the latter, on joining the family circle, produced a small volume which he said his friend Mr. Pierce had just given him, as the work of a young author in whom he took a special interest and in whose future he had great faith. It was the *Twice Told Tales* of Nathaniel Hawthorne.

President Pierce speedily and thoroughly disappointed the hopes of his old friend and of all the Northern Democrats who had taken part in the Free-Soil movement of 1848. His congratulations to the country in his first Annual Message, December 5, 1853, on the repose and security in the public mind created by the compromise measures, coupled with the declaration that " this repose is to suffer no shock during my official term, if I have power to avert it," were followed, before the end of the same month, by the measure introduced in the Senate as a part of the Kansas–Nebraska bill, to repeal the Missouri compromise of 1820, a bold and concerted plan by which the leaders of the Democratic party, South and North, declared their deliberate adhesion to the Slave Power and its aggressive policy. The shock of this traitorous blow at the compact by which slavery had been restricted from the territory now about to be embraced in the Union, ended all further repose on compromises, earlier or later, awoke as with a trumpet blast the free spirit of the North, and heralded the opening of the final struggle between sectionalism and the Nation.

At the great meeting of citizens held in the City Hall Park, May 15, 1854, to protest, on the eve of its final passage, against the bill repealing the Missouri compromise, the principal speech was made by Mr. Butler, who though enfeebled by recent illness, spoke, in the open air, to five thousand people, with all his wonted vigor and fire, striking the key-note of the speedy harmony and united action which welded together in the Republican party all the opposing forces rallied against slavery extension, when he declared that the issue must be joined upon this attempted subversion of the ancient ordinance of freedom, and that if for example, Stephen Arnold Douglas, its leading Northern promoter, "were a candidate for President to-day, nominated by a Baltimore Convention, and William H. Seward or any other honest man were the candidate of the opponents of this bill, he should vote for William H. Seward if it were the last thing he had to do in this sublunary sphere."

The force of this declaration, received with wild enthusiasm, was well understood at the time and nothing could more forcibly express the breaking up of all old party issues and alliances in the new emergency which rallied men, hitherto widely apart in political opinion, to the standard of revolt against the invasions of the Slave Power.

From that time, he was constant and conspicuous in his efforts against the steady aggressions and outrages of the slavery propagandists. He voted for Fremont in 1856, and by voice as well as vote denounced the frauds and crimes involved in the effort to fasten slavery upon the people of Kansas. Still, with many other men of those troublous times, he did not anticipate a violent issue of the conflict, but hoped to the end of his life for a peaceful solution by constitutional methods. "Never despair of the right. Tyrants and apostates may attempt what they please. They may endeavor to bear down the rights of the people, but all their assaults will be in vain in the presence of a free, intelligent people like those of the Free States." These words spoken in the Park in 1854, were prophetic of results reached in a way he did not foresee. He was not spared to witness their complete fulfillment, but had the scriptural portion accorded to the good man "taken away from the evil to come."

The later years of his professional life were largely given to a litigation of great magnitude which grew out of the attempt of the representatives of an insolvent corporation, the North American Trust and Banking Company, one of the speculative enterprises of which the financial history of New York has presented so many specimens, to defeat the claims of its secured creditors, chiefly English capitalists.

The amounts involved in the various suits which arose in the cause of this litigation and which during many years were pending in the courts of this State, do not, in these later days of gigantic corporate obligations appear as startling as they did in that earlier time. The validity of trusts, one known as the Million Trust, and others as the Half Million Trusts were the main subjects of dispute, but the complexity of the facts, the novelty and importance of the questions involved and the singular zeal and ability with which the opposition to the creditors was conducted, combined to make the various suits almost unparalleled in their number and in the methods by which they were promoted. On the opposing sides of these cases the ablest lawyers in the State were ranged against each other. As leading counsel for the English creditors, among whom were the Bank of England and other capitalists in London, Mr. Butler had the largest share of the labor and responsibility of the contest and this, at a time when he was broken in heart and spirit by the death, in the summer of 1853, of his wife, a blow from which he never recovered and which, with his arduous self-imposed professional task, broke down his vigorous constitution.

Of one instance of his labors in these causes Judge Kent says :

" In this case which for voluminous and complicated pleadings and proofs was perhaps unparalleled in our Courts, it was deemed necessary that a condensed statement of the evidence of the whole case and legal points, with minute references to the proofs and authorities affecting every point, should be prepared for the Court of Appeals. Two of the associated lawyers were prevented by other engagements from undertaking the work ; I shrunk from it as utterly beyond my powers—and it fell to the self-sacrificing industry of Mr. Butler. Our conferences in relation to it were of daily occurrence, and I observed, with alarm, its gradual effect upon his health. Often have I left him bending over his desk, late of a July night, and found him the next morning in the same posture, which had been varied, in the interval, by only a brief period of intermission, in which he has told me that sleep was often sought in vain. I remonstrated often, seriously—almost angrily. I remember his once answering me by repeating Wordsworth's ' Ode to Duty.' It was impossible to withdraw him from his work ; and thus health was wasted at the midnight taper—life itself consumed in the severe labors of his office—and when his task was finished to the admiration of his associates and opponents, the anxious eye of friendship saw too surely that the stamina of his constitution was gone. It enhances our idea of his energy, to know that this too protracted labor was in part performed while mourning a bereavement, the most afflicting that could occur to a man of his domestic affections. I have no right, even in the spirit of panegyric, to invade the privacy of his domestic affections ; but it is not improper to say that the loss of the beloved and honored partner of his life gave additional effect to his fatal labor, while our admiration is increased when we think that he carried on his work, enduring in silence and composure a heartfelt wound which had touched a nerve where "agony resided."

Such was the importance of the case to which Judge Kent refers, that the Court of Appeals gave to its hearing an entire term. Probably no such forensic contest ever occurred in this State, or is likely to occur in the future, as that whose result is embodied in the first two hundred and ninety-seven pages of the fifteenth volume of the New York Reports. Greene C. Bronson and Samuel Beardsley, two of the foremost jurists in the State, only lately retired from the Bench of the Supreme Court, and Nicholas Hill, in many respects the best equipped lawyer at the Bar, were opposed to Benjamin F. Butler, Charles O'Conor, William Kent and William Curtis Noyes. Besides these noted names which appear in the report, other able lawyers had been concerned in the management and preparation of the case, and no subject of controversy was ever more skilfully or completely presented to a Court of Justice.

The fourteen resolutions of the Court disposing of the question involved in favor of the English creditors was a signal victory for their counsel and a crowning professional triumph for their senior, who was well satisfied to associate with the close of his long professional career, a success in the interest of justice, against what he regarded as a scheme of repudiation and wrong.

In spite of exhausted strength and failing health he was induced to enter upon another, and as it proved a final, professional contest, in which his personal sympathies and his sense of justice were enlisted in behalf of a client whose cause he espoused as if it were his own.

Uriah P. Levy, a captain in the United States Navy, who had risen in the service by his gallantry and efficiency, had been a comrade in the war of 1812 of Lieut. William Howard Allen, of whom mention has already been made. A fellow prisoner with him at one time, it was a tradition of their captivity that they were given the privilege of walking from their place of confinement as far as a certain mile-stone on the road leading into the interior country. Taking advantage of the solitude or the darkness in one of their walks, they dug up the mile-stone and removed it to a considerable distance inland, thus securing a substantial enlargement of the jail liberties.

This fellowship of suffering and adventure with one whom my father had loved and mourned as a brother, made Captain Levy a welcome guest at his house, and was deemed to entitle him to the self-sacrificing service which he invoked to secure redress against the oppression and injustice of the government to which he had devoted his life.

Levy was an Israelite. His personal bearing was not agreeable to his fellow-officers. They objected to him on the ground of his race and his manners, and occasions of complaint and provocation arose whereever he was placed on duty. He had been arraigned before six several courts martial for improprieties of conduct, most of them trivial, and had received and submitted to several sentences, comparatively light, until, by the judgment of the sixth court martial, he was dismissed from the service of the United States. Upon a review, this harsh sentence was disapproved by President Tyler and Commodore Levy retained his command and rank, but such was the prejudicy against him that he was unable to induce the Navy Department to assign him to any post of duty. Finally, under the operation of an Act of Congress, passed in 1855, "to promote the efficiency of the Navy," a Board of fifteen officers reported him to the Secretary of the Navy for dismissal, and his name was stricken from the roll. This action was without notice to Levy or opportunity of hearing, and was based mainly on the records of the six courts martial of which he had been the subject, although the last of these had taken place, and its sentence had been annulled, nearly fifteen years before the action of the Board, and although he was in full vigor of mind and body, and competent for every duty of his captaincy.

Smarting under this injustice, and after having appealed in vain to the Navy Department, Levy, who was possessed of ample means and of untiring energy, devoted himself to the task of procuring redress by legal methods, and, after ong and patient effort, succeeded in procuring, as a necessary basis for a review of his case, the passage, in January, 1857, of an Act of Congress establishing a Court of Inquire to investigate the case of any officer dismissed by the Board of Fifteen, and to report thereon.

A day in court being thus accorded, Levy, with the aid of his counsel, made good his claim for a thorough investigation. All the records of the previous courts affecting him were ransacked, his whole career was made the subject of scrutiny and evidence, and, after a long and arduous trial, the overwhelming mass of testimony compelled a finding by the Court in his favor, and a report that he ought to be restored to the active list with the grade of Captain. The President having approved this finding, he was nominated to the Senate, and confirmed by that body, as Captain, from the 29th of March, 1844, a restoration to rank and vindication of character, as complete as it was unique, in the history of the Naval Service.

Nothing short of the most painstaking and thorough efforts could possibly have sufficed to overcome the deeply rooted prejudices which had been the foundation of this long and active persecution directed against a competent and faithful officer. The defense of Captain Levy as prepared and published with the annexed proceedings and testimony, was the last important work done by his friend and counsel, and is a signal illustration of what may be accomplished, by patience and skill, in reversing wrong judgments and vindicating right principles.

After the completion of this final work, on October 16, 1858, my father sailed from New York in the steamer "Arago," accompanied by his two youngest daughters, and intending to spend two years in travel and residence in Europe. He arrived at Havre October 29th, and after a short stay at Rouen, reached Paris, where he was taken ill almost immediately, and where he died at the Hotel du Louvre, November 8, 1858, aged sixty-two years, ten months and twenty-five days.

At the meeting of American citizens in Paris on the occasion of his death, John Y. Mason of Virginia, then United States Minister to France, afterwards conspicuous in the memorable Mason and Slidell incident of the Rebellion, presided, and Hamilton Fish, already eminent in public life, and in later years the wise and efficient administrator of the State Department, presented the resolutions. On the eve of their bitter struggle the North and South united by leading representatives of each section in a tribute of respect to a man justly eulogized by both for his services to his native State and to the whole country.

At home the tributes of the Bar, at the meeting held December 1, 1858, to which reference has been already made in the sketch of the Revision and at the funeral services December 2, 1858, were of a remarkable character, both as to the speakers and the words they spoke. Mr. Justice Nelson of the Supreme Court of the United States, long our ideal in bearing, manner and every element of judicial fitness, was the presiding officer of the meeting of the Bar. Samuel J. Tilden, conspicuous then and always for his clear insight and great professional and political sagacity; Judge Kent, a man of rare accomplishments and the finest sympathies; Marshall S. Bidwell, a jurist affluent in learning and of high christian character; Judge Edmonds, noted for his fearlessness in the discharge of duty, and his enthusiasm in every cause he deemed a righteous one; Daniel Lord, the type and fit exemplar of the commercial lawyer in the highest sense, a representative of all that was best in the great metropolis of the Nation, united in terms of eulogy which would seem extravagant and overcolored if their truth were not attested by the strong, unmistakable personal emotion which marked their utterances. When Judge Kent, in his address, unexcelled for beauty and grace by any effort of the class to which it belongs, said in closing:—"If, to a stranger, this imperfect sketch of the friend we mourn shall appear to be too unmingled a eulogy, I can only say that I believe I have been attempting to describe a man in whom I knew no fault,"—he spoke in full memory of the many years during which he had been in close contact with that friend in many sharp and bitter contests, in all of which the scrutiny of unbiased and manly observers found him always sincere in friendship, loyal in duty, pure in life and unselfish in purpose.

The religious side of his character which was marked by the same thoroughness and fidelity which belonged to his professional career was emphasized almost as fully by the judges and lawyers I have named as by the clergymen who spoke at his burial. Doctor William B. Sprague of Albany, a divine of national reputation ; Doctor Thomas H. Skinner long the revered pastor of the Mercer Street Church in New York ; Doctor William Adams the learned and beloved minister of the Madison Square Presbyterian Church, later the head of the Union Theological Seminary, and George W. Bethune, foremost in the pulpit of the Reformed Church for eloquence and ability, and no stranger to platforms where public questions of the hour needed his ringing, stirring tones, all spoke in words prompted by long association and close friendship, alike in commendation although very various in expression and illustration.

These, in their turn, might seem overstrained were it not for the warmth and vividness which made them the testimony not only of willing but of truthful witnesses. "He was a man," said Doctor Bethune, in the single passage I transcribe from these memorial addresses, "whose piety was his life. My dear mother said to me, once, of a person I had spoken well of ; ' My son, he puts on his politeness as he does his best coat. Give me a man whose politeness is in his skin !' So it was in Mr. Butler's religion. It was part of himself. There was no affectation about it. No one ever supposed there was. It shone out of that bright eye, can it be that bright eye will never shine on us again ? It beamed from his countenance, it came from his heart, it was a transfiguration from within that made his life so beautiful in all the grace and kindness of a christian gentleman."

To these testimonies I need hardly add my own.

The record I have traced barely indicates the wide and varied character of the labors of the life to which it relates, and wholly fails to exhibit the personal traits which gave to every aspect of that life and work their own peculiar charm.

Few men were ever more fully and constantly occupied in weighty matters of private and public concern, or more keenly sensitive to the responsibilities they imposed. This made him habitually serious, but never disturbed the even cheerfulness which was his habit of mind, or deprived him of the pleasure to be gained by turning from the drudgery of his daily tasks to the delights of home, the recreations of literature, the society of friends, or the companionship of Nature. His rare liberality and catholicity of spirit and the regard for the rights of all men, religious, social and political, which he carried into practice with a rare consistency and consideration, kept him singularly free from personal asperities even in the heated party conflicts in which he sometimes found himself opposed to friends and associates ; and he harbored no resentments against men who had done him cruel and malicious wrong. This nobility of character was a trait which endeared him to a host of true friends in different walks of life and of widely divergent views and beliefs.

He was deeply and sincerely religious ; a rare specimen of true piety without a trace of bigotry or even of sectarianism, for he was as catholic in his faith as he was humane in his sympathies. I cannot exaggerate or overstate my sense of his virtues, which were the fruit and flower of divine grace working in a nature which seemed responsive to its heavenly touch to a degree seldom seen in the sons of men.

His grave is at Woodlawn Cemetery, and on the stone which marks it are carved, according to his own direction, beside the Scripture text which attests his Christian faith and trust, and a record of his services in the Cabinets of Jackson and Van Buren, these words, commemorative of his share in the greatest work of his life : " A COMMISSIONER TO REVISE THE STATUTE LAWS OF THE STATE OF NEW YORK."